The Best Places
To Kiss™
In New York City

Other Books in The Best Places To Kiss . . . Series

The Best Places To Kiss In The Northwest
The Best Places To Kiss In San Francisco — Revised*
The Best Places To Kiss In Los Angeles
The Best Places To Kiss In Southern California*
                    ***(Available fall 1989)**

The Best Places To Kiss™ In New York City

by **Paula Begoun**

Beginning Press

Managing Editor: Sheree Bykofsky
Art Direction & Production: Constance Bollen
Cover Design: Rob Pawlak
Typography: Common Line Communications
Copy Editor: Shellie Tucker
Printing: Bookcrafters
Contributors: Sheree Bykofsky, Jack Eichenbaum, Gerry McTigue, Linda Gruber, Carol Milano, Mark SaFranko, Piri Halasz, Audrey Kurland, Heidi Atlas, Doug Hoyt, Walter Alexander, Linda Lewin, Adam O'Connor, Karyn Feiden, Susan Carr, Alison Brown Cerier, Paul Fargis, Sue Katz

This book may be ordered directly from the publisher:
5418 So. Brandon, Seattle, WA 98118

Please include $9.95 ($12.95 Canadian) plus $1.50 postage and handling.

PROFESSIONAL THANK YOUS

The most heartfelt gratitude to Sheree Bykofsky, whose enthusiastic support and reliable professionalism made this venture easier (well, *relatively easier*) than I ever hoped could be possible. Thanks also to Barbara Murel and Michael Hofferbert for their continued skill and patience, Constance Bollen for her book designing expertise and Shellie Tucker for her copyediting ability.

SPECIAL ACKNOWLEDGEMENTS

To my creative sister, Avis Begoun, for the original idea, my dear friends Jim Joseph and Judy Wagh, and my generous other sister, Channa Druxman, for the use of their respective homes as a base camp in New York City; Channa and Jeremy Staiman and Abe Sheiden for their love and support; and to all the starry-eyed people who let me interview them about their favorite kissing places.

PUBLISHER'S NOTE

This book is not an advertising vehicle. As was true in all the **Best Places To Kiss** books, none of the businesses included here was told it either was being considered or had been chosen for inclusion; establishments were neither charged fees nor did they pay us. No services were exchanged. This book is a sincere effort to highlight those special parts of the area that are filled with romance and splendor. Sometimes those places are created by people, as in restaurants, inns, lounges, lodges, hotels and bed & breakfasts. Sometimes those places are untouched by people and simply created by God for us to enjoy.

The recommendations in this collection were the final decision of the author and editors. Please write to Beginning Press if you have any additional comments, suggestions or recommendations.

"As usual with most lovers in the city —
they were troubled by the lack of that
essential need of love — a meeting place."

Thomas Wolfe

DEDICATION

To my husband, who keeps telling me that the best place to kiss is at home with him, curled up in front of the fireplace.

> "LOVE DOESN'T MAKE THE WORLD GO AROUND —
> IT'S WHAT MAKES THE RIDE WORTHWHILE."
>
> *Franklin P. Jones*

TABLE OF CONTENTS

> "IN LITERATURE, AS IN LOVE, WE ARE ASTONISHED
> AT WHAT IS CHOSEN BY OTHERS."
>
> *Andre Maurois*

KISSING 104

Why Is It Best To Kiss In New York City?

I've wondered about that notion, why it's best to kiss in a particular city, from the moment I started writing this series of romantic travel guides. I began with the original Pacific Northwest kissing book three years ago (it has since been updated), and I have completed three others, one for the Los Angeles area, one for San Francisco and now this one for New York City. In each area I ask this same question and hope that before I'm done, I will have found an answer.

It seems that writing about romance and romantic places in New York has involved the trickiest research of all. I knew I was in trouble from the very start, with my initial two interviews. The first interviewee told me that the best place to kiss was at his apartment, and he proceeded to give me his card with directions printed on the back. (It dawned on me at that point that randomly asking men might be more of a problem than it was worth.) The second person I interviewed, logically a woman, said that the best place to kiss in New York City was on a plane to the Caribbean or any point several hundred miles north, south, east or west of here. The next dozen respondents weren't any better. They suggested crowded, well-known, touristy spots, or they described restaurants that required a second mortgage just to look at the menu, or worse, they had ideas about romance I simply couldn't fathom. (If there is anyone here who likes to kiss at the city dump or morgue, you're in the wrong book.)

As I walked dejectedly up 5th Avenue just past 64th Street, in the midst of one of the worst cases of writer's block I've ever experienced, I thought of what a confusing romantic location New York City is. Far be it from me to remind an already over-reminded New Yorker that this city is a series of unnerving contradictions — the best and worst of everything — but the truth is the truth:

New York is beautiful/frightening, friendly/unsafe, glittery/seamy, luxurious/poverty stricken, exciting/? . . . ! Okay, that's it! That's the part of New York City that doesn't have a contradiction, what lies at the very heart of the matter. New York City's allure is its intensity, diversity and basic eclectic eccentricity.

Where else, on the second day of my research — after a leisurely breakfast at Le Regence, a peaceful morning buggy ride through Central Park, a romp through F.A.O. Schwarz with an ice cream sundae chaser at Rumpelmayers, an elegant early-evening glass of champagne at the Petrossian Room, a relaxing dinner at Trattoria Dell'Arte, a Broadway musical finished with a properly foamed cappuccino at the Top of the Towers — could I witness an errant individual relieving himself, not once but twice, on the building I was passing; have a very deranged young person try to hold my hand; and have no less than four raving subway car orators and six miscellaneous religious fanatics of varying unidentified affiliations ask me for money after pouring their tragic, albeit drug-and-crime-free, life stories into my ear?

So, why is it best to kiss in New York City? Because there is indeed an incomparable excitement that accompanies everything you do here. You can feel it as you wander (*carefully*) through the parks, along the avenues and in and out of the shops and restaurants. When you're in New York you feel as if you're at the center of the world, actually aware that it doesn't get any more fascinating than this. And, when you have each other, plus limitless romantic options at your beck and call and mile after mile of sights and sounds abounding in this adult carnival of a city, what else do you need? Well, maybe blindfolds; you may on occasion need blindfolds to avoid looking too closely at some of the excitement that isn't even vaguely romantic. Okay, okay, and money; you do need some money, but after that, it's all up to you and your own personal kissing preferences.

Note: When you're in New York City, nothing outside of it exists. The world drops off abruptly just west of the Hudson River — but not as far as this book is concerned. Those New Yorkers who know where to find trees and lakes and quiet understand an inner peace that keeps the hectic pace here from getting the better of them. And here are some of their secrets on getting out of the city and into the country in two hours or less.

You Call This Research?

This book was undertaken primarily as a journalistic effort. It was the collaborative work of a group of New York writers and is the product of earnest interviews, travel, careful investigation and observation.

Although it would have been nice, actually even preferable, kissing was not used as the major research method for selecting the locations listed in this book. If smooching had been the determining factor, several inescapable problems would have resulted. First, I assure you, we would still be researching, and this book would be just a good idea, some random notes and nothing more. And second, depending on the two researchers' moods of the moment, many kisses would have occurred in a lot of places that do not meet the requirements of this travel guide. Therefore, for both practical and physical reasons, more objective criteria had to be established (except for my very romantically inclined managing editor, who I think did kiss at every location she reviewed).

You may be wondering, if we all did not kiss at every location during our research, how could any of us be certain if a particular place was good for such an activity? My sincere answer is that a more intuitive reporter's instinct was employed to evaluate the magnetic, heartfelt pull of each place visited. The ultimate criterion, in addition to those listed below, was that if, upon examining a place, the reviewer felt a longing inside for his or her special someone to share what had been discovered, that was considered as reliable a test as kissing. In the final analysis, I can guarantee that once you choose where to go from among any of the places listed, you will be assured of some amount of privacy, a beautiful setting, a heart-stirring ambience and first-rate accommodations. When you get there, what you do romantically is up to you and your partner.

What Isn't Romantic

You may be skeptical about the idea of one location being more romantic than another. You may think, *"Well, it isn't the setting, it's who you're with that makes a place special."* And you'd be right. But aside from the chemistry that exists between the two of you, which is all its own, there are some locations that can add to the moment, as opposed to some you're best off pretending don't exist.

For example, holding hands over a hamburger and fries at McDonald's, or sharing a slice of pizza while waiting for your train, might be, for some, a blissful interlude. But the french-fry fight in full swing near your heads, the preoccupied youth who took a year and a day to get your order or the guy sleeping in front of the entrance can put a damper on heartthrob stuff even for the most adoring of us. No, location isn't everything; it's just that when a certain type of place is combined with all the right details, including the right person, you have better odds of romance happening unhindered and uninterrupted.

With that in mind, the following is a list of things that were never considered to be even remotely romantic: olive green or orange carpeting (especially if it was mildewy or dirty), anything overly plastic or overly veneered, an abundance of neon (even if it was very art deco or very neo-modern), most tourist traps, restaurants with no-smoking sections who ignored their own policy, over-priced hotels with impressive names and mediocre accommodations, discos, the latest need-to-be-seen-in nightspots (romantic places only count when the most important person there is you and not someone at the table across the room), restaurants with officious, sneering waiters, and last, but not least, a roomful of people discussing the stock market and Donald Trump's latest acquisition.

Above and beyond these unromantic location details, there is a small variety of unromantic behaviors that can negate the affection potential of the most majestic surroundings. The following are mood killers every time: any amount of moaning over the weather; creating a scene over the quality of food or service, no matter how justified; worrying about work; getting angry about traffic; incessant back-seat driving, no matter how warranted; complaining about heartburn and other related symptoms, even if painful or justified.

Rating Romance

The three major factors determining whether a place would be included were:

1. **Surrounding splendor**
2. **Privacy**
3. **Tug-at-your-heartstrings ambience**

This one-of-a-kind rating system was used as follows: if a place had all three of those qualities going for it, inclusion was automatic. But if one or two of the criteria were weak or nonexistent, the other feature(s) had to be really incredible before the location would be included. For example, if a panoramic vista was breathtakingly beautiful in a spot that was inundated with tourists and children on field trips, the place would not be included. Or, if a fabulous bed & breakfast was set in a less-than-desirable location, it would be included if and only if its interior was so wonderfully inviting and cozy that the outside no longer mattered.

Of the three determining factors, "*surrounding splendor*" is fairly self-explanatory. "*Heart-tugging ambience*" could probably use some clarification: wonderful, loving environments are not just four-poster beds covered with down quilts and lace pillows, or tables decorated with white tablecloths and nicely folded linen napkins. Instead there must be more plush or engaging features that encourage you to feel relaxed and carefree rather than rigid and formal. For the most part, ambience was always judged by comfort and gracious appointments as opposed to image and frills. The last item, *"privacy,"* requires a section unto itself, as in the next paragraph.

Kiss Ratings

If you've flipped through this book and noticed the miniature lips that follow each entry, you may be curious about their implications. The rating system notwithstanding, **ALL** the listings in this book are wonderful, special places to be, and all of them have heart-pleasing details, are worthwhile and enticing. The tiny lips only indicate our personal preferences and nothing more. They are a way of indicating just how delightfully romantic a place was and how pleased we were with the experience during our visit. The number of lips awarded each location corresponds as follows:

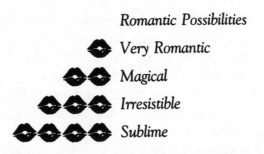

Romantic Possibilities

Very Romantic

Magical

Irresistible

Sublime

Rating Cost

There are also additional ratings to help you determine whether your lips can afford to kiss in a particular restaurant, hotel or bed & breakfast (almost all of the outdoor places are free or require a reasonably small charge). The price for overnight accommodations is always based on double occupancy; otherwise there wouldn't be anyone to kiss. Eating-establishment prices are based on a full dinner for two, excluding liquor, unless otherwise indicated. Because of the tendency for prices and business hours to change, it is always advised that you call and double-check the present status of each place you consider visiting so that your lips do not end up disappointed.

Restaurant Rating

Inexpensive — $25-$40
Moderate — $40-$65
Expensive — $65-$100
Very Expensive — $100-$150
Very, Very Expensive and beyond — $150 and up

Hotel/Lodging Rating

Inexpensive — Under $85
Moderate — $85-$135
Expensive — $135-$225
Very Expensive — $225-$350
Very, Very Expensive and beyond — $350 and up

What If You Don't Want To Kiss?

One resistance many of the people I interviewed had to the idea of best kissing locales stemmed from their expectation worries. Some people were apprehensive that they'd travel to these places and, once they arrived, never get the feeling they thought they were supposed to have. They imagined spending all that time setting up the plans and getting ready, heading out for the promised land and then — after negotiating in unexpected traffic with surly cab drivers, arriving late, finding the prices had increased exponentially and the people next to them were loud and obnoxious (even for New York) — not being swept away in a flourish of romance. Their understandable fear was, what happens if nothing happens?

Having experienced those situations more than once in my life, I empathize, but I'm prepared with solutions. Part of the problem can occur in the planning stage. To prevent an anticlimactic scenario, consider some suggestions that might just help you survive a romantic outing: When you make decisions about where and when to go, pay close attention to details; talk over your preferences and discuss your feelings about them. For some people there is no passion associated with pre-theatre fast dinners that are all but inhaled, walking farther than expected in overly high heels, or finding a place closed because their hours have changed. Another consideration is the never-ending dilemma of trying to second-guess traffic patterns in New York. My strong recommendation, although I know this one is hard: Do not schedule a romantic outing too tightly or you will be more assured of a headache than an affectionate interlude. How different factors might affect your lips, not to mention your mood, is something to agree on before you head out the door, not after.

In spite of all that, it is important to remember that part of the whole experience of an intimate time together is allowing whatever happens to be an opportunity to let affection reign. Regardless of what takes place, that is what is romantic. For example, remember the film *Body Heat*, and the incredibly intense scene where Kathleen Turner is standing in the hall and William Hurt smashes through the door (even though it appears to be unlocked) and rushes into her waiting arms, tumbling them both to the floor? Well, how romantic would it have been if Kathleen had started fretting about having to clean up the broken glass, get the door fixed and repair her torn underwear? Or remember the scene on the beach between Deborah Kerr and Burt Lancaster in *From Here to Eternity*, where they're rolling around passionately in the surf? How much kissing would they have gotten to if Burt had started complaining about the water up his nose, the sand down his bathing suit and the arctic chill in the air? Get the idea?

So, if the car breaks down, the train stops between stations for what seems like a lifetime, the waiter is rude to you, your reservations get screwed up, or both of you tire out and want to call it a day, you can still be endearing and charming. It really only takes an attitude change to turn any dilemma into a delight.

Warm Heart, Cold Feet, Empty Wallet

More than in almost any other area of the United States, romance in New York City can cost money and a lot of it. As a New York friend would frequently remind me, he couldn't walk out of his apartment without spending an unreasonable amount of money. And it never failed, when he got back home flat broke and with no tangible items to justify his poverty, in a semi-dazed state he would always wonder aloud, *"Where did it all go?"* I hate to be an optimist in the face of a depressing truism, but it doesn't have to be as bad as my friend makes it sound. Not that it can't be absurdly expensive to run around here and enjoy yourself, but it can be tempered with a little self-reliance and budgeting. (This is the Jewish Mother part of the book.) Of course, if you have unlimited resources, you can skip over this section and proceed to the next.

PROBLEM: You want to go out for the evening to someplace intimate and wonderful, but the cost is prohibitive. **SOLUTION:** Rather than going out for dinner, go at an off-time to your dream restaurant and enjoy an appetizer and a beverage or dessert and tea. Then go home and split a large cheese pizza from Ray's with a little gelati for dessert.

PROBLEM: The theatre as an evening out is a great idea, but you can't afford that plus the car fare and after-theatre food and drinks. **SOLUTION:** The myriad of cabarets and jazz clubs that offer great entertainment for under $10 per person, particularly the ones listed in this book, often have romantic environments. Also there are half-priced theatre tickets to be found at the **TKTS booth, 354-5800,** *on 47th and Broadway,* or **2 World Trade Center**

mezzanine, the day of the performance, if you're willing to stand in line for an hour or so. There are also Off-Off Broadway shows that are significantly less expensive than Broadway ones. A music and dance half-price tickets booth, **382-2323**, can be found at *Bryant Park, on 42nd Street between 5th and 6th Avenues.*

PROBLEM: Fancy restaurants are great, but I get hives dressing up. **SOLUTION:** Afternoon tea at many of the hotels that line Central Park is a wonderful way to spend a dressed down, elegant few hours relatively inexpensively.

PROBLEM: You want to spend the weekend someplace really romantic, and that doesn't mean at the apartment, but most of the nice hotels charge as much as you're paying for rent. **SOLUTION:** Call the bed & breakfast service listed in the Hotel/Lodging section. They offer incredible getaways for $125 or less a night, including breakfast and, sometimes, amenities such as a Jacuzzi, views or a king-size bed with thick goose-down comforters.

In the long run, this is a vast region with wonderful nooks and crannies that at any time of year can be safe havens where the two of you can share precious time together, without spending a penny except on transportation. From brisk hikes in the country to long strolls along the avenues, peaceful sunsets in the park, flower markets to browse in and country roads to explore out on Long Island or in Westchester, a range of magic places hovers close by for you to enjoy. Your togetherness, and this book, will enhance that magic.

"THE SOUND OF A KISS IS NOT SO LOUD

AS THAT OF A CANNON — BUT ITS ECHO LASTS

A GREAT DEAL LONGER."

Oliver Wendell Holmes, Sr.

◆ Hotel Kissing ◆

BED & BREAKFAST NEW YORK CITY STYLE
Urban Ventures
594-5650
Inexpensive to Moderate

Urban Ventures is a service that is unique to New York City. They list hundreds of locations all over the city that I would define loosely as bed & breakfast accommodations. It's not that they're not bed & breakfasts; they're just not the sort you may have encountered elsewhere in the world. If you're only familiar with the assortment of Victorian mansions and private homes in the U.S. that have been renovated to accommodate the needs of those who have had enough of hotel vacationing, then let me inform you that Manhattan doesn't have those. Here people with extra living space (in a city with very little extra space) rent out those bedrooms — some with private baths — and they vary in style from basic to extravagant. But for less than $100 a night we've never been disappointed, unlike with hotels in the same price range, and it has always proven to be a real adventure.

Once the resident handed us the keys to his huge East Side loft. It was attractive and convenient, and it felt like we were living there. No hotel clerks, no room service charges, the kitchen was right there and so was a nearby Chinese restaurant that delivered. The apartment was very high-tech, equipped with a remarkable stereo system. Another time we stayed with a charming couple, whose own bedroom was at the other end of their co-op, and they personally served us a lavish breakfast.

Urban Ventures has over 700 listings and the variations on a theme are endless, but let me make a few recommendations to help make your stay a positive adventure: Be specific about check-in and check-out times; have the space where you will be staying described in detail; ask about size, private bath, smoking, kids, method of entry, location, food served if any, cancellation policy, type of bed, doorman building, walkup or elevator and whether cash or a charge card is acceptable.

I know that might sound more complicated than a hotel, but if you are interested in an alternative, whether it be for business or romance, and especially if your tastes are more expensive than what your budget can afford, then staying in a bed & breakfast, Manhattan style, can be a truly unique experience.

THE BOX TREE HOTEL and RESTAURANT
250 East 49th Street *between 2nd & 3rd Avenues*
PL8-8320
Very Expensive

The lip ratings are designed to indicate quality based on a four-kiss system, but if I had enough room to go higher, I would easily attribute 10, no make that 100, lips for this ornate, superlative example of regal, grandly ostentatious living and eating. No, make that feasting and residing in heaven. But, alas, the lip rating is simply a privacy rating. How, then, do I let you know that this is a better place than almost any other in Manhattan to kiss, sleep, relax, eat, soak, read, talk and just about anything else you can do inside.

The outside gives no hint of what lies inside. But all that melts into oblivion once you pass from the real world into theirs. I prefer theirs. Perhaps it will impress you as a European villa or a miniature Versailles or the wild imagination of owner Augustin Paege or all three, which is probably closest to the truth. The 15 rooms are palatial in style and with an extravagance beyond compare. From the Chinese Suite to the King Boris Bedroom to the Consulate Suite, each is finished in a provocative abundance of gold chandeliers, marble and lapis lazuli baths (*yes, in the bath*), marble-mantled, working fireplaces, antique screens and plush furnishings. And the restaurant showcases the same attention to lavish detail as the hotel, with the stupendous talents of a kitchen that prepares and serves a prix fixe lunch and dinner as amazing as your surroundings.

Note: If you're staying in the hotel ($240 – $290 a night for a double), they will give you a $100 credit toward your dinner in the hotel, which is prix fixe at $76 (lunch is $37). Now that's what I call living on love the right way.

THE LOWELL HOTEL
28 East 63rd Street *between 5th & Madison Avenues*
838-1400
Very Expensive and Beyond

Generally you can assume that most of the city's hotels are designed to efficiently handle large groups of people or to encourage business people to take care of business. Every now and then, there is the exception to the rule and slick is replaced with elegance and efficiency is embellished with warmth and beauty in every corner of the establishment. The Lowell is all those things and more. The furnishings are exquisite and supremely comfortable, with an eye for blending textures and colors. There are even wood-burning fireplaces framed by painstakingly renovated mantles. The bathrooms are a bit on the small side. I prefer bathtubs large enough to serve dinner in, but the marble surfaces and amenities help obscure that problem. This is one of my absolutely favorite New York places to hide out in for a while.

◆ *Romantic Suggestion:* Even if the Lowell Hotel weren't so splendid, **The Pembroke Room** would be reason enough to pay a visit here. This room is a radiant composite of a restaurant and tea room. The prodigious dining environment is very English, very civilized, very distinguished and richly adorned. You'll feel as if you were residing in a countryside estate near Suffolk. The cuisine is inspired, with an emphasis on presentation and kid-glove service. I can't think of a more romantic location to partake of breakfast, lunch or tea. Their Sunday brunch is equally fabulous and equally expensive.

THE PENINSULA HOTEL
700 5th Avenue *at 55th Street*
247-2200
Very Expensive and Beyond

There are plenty of attractive hotels in New York City, from the Grand Hyatt with its slick greenhouse setting to the Waldorf Astoria's Victorian charm and old-world appeal, but most of the space and beauty of this city's hotels seem to exist only in the lobby and restaurants. The rooms are, unfortunately, just hotel rooms, nothing special or extraordinary, with bathrooms that border on small, and nothing is less romantic than a small bathroom.

These drawbacks are far from the case, however, at the Peninsula Hotel. For the same extravagant price as most of the other hotels, the Peninsula offers huge, elegant suites in tones of peach and rose with wonderful king-size beds. And the bathrooms all feature oversized six-foot tubs large enough for a small crowd, but two is enough. Now that's my kind of hotel room. Their weekend packages tempt even budgeting couples in the mood for mutual self- indulgence or a special anniversary weekend.

♦ *Romantic Warning:* The second-floor restaurant and bar are nice but very expensive and not particularly worth it.

PLAZA ATHENEE & LE REGENCE
37th East 64th Street *between Park & Madison Avenues*
734-9100
Very Expensive and Beyond

After weeks of wandering in and out of the myriad hotels lining the streets and avenues of Manhattan, I was relieved to find the

Hotel Athenee. I was beginning to doubt that I would find anything that met the criteria for romantic accommodations. Most of what I saw were little more than standard hotel rooms, and many, even the supremely expensive ones surrounding Central Park, bordered on tacky. Their lobbies were gorgeous, the restaurants and cocktail lounges dazzling and refined, which would be perfect if that's where I could sleep, but when I saw the suites, well, I was no longer tired. And then I wandered into the Hotel Athenee. The rooms, even the simple ones, were charming, but the two on the top floor were exquisite, and in comparison with most of everything else in the area, completely romantic.

The entryway was large and encased in mirrors. The room itself was spacious with a king-size four-poster bed and soft linens and a quilt. And then there was the bathroom. A sexy bathroom can take any ordinary room and make it dynamite. A sexy bathroom plus a beautiful room is positively enthralling. The whole room is lovingly made for two: the gold-colored marble floors, ceilings and walls, and the huge walk-in shower. Plus if you decide to venture out of your room and you don't want to go too far, the incredibly precious and opulent restaurant Le Regence is available for breakfast, lunch or dinner. It is worth it to forgo room service just to have this dining experience. The velvety smooth, forest green bar adjacent to Le Regence assuredly warrants toasting time secretly spent together.

THE ROYALTON
44 West 44th Street *between Park & 6th Avenues*
869-4400
Very Expensive to Very, Very Expensive

Of all the entries in this collection, this one has caused the most controversy and frustration, for two reasons. First, the Royalton started off its questionably illustrious beginnings (October '88) with a discrimination suit (the hotel settled out of court) and second, it seems apparent that the staff has been trained to never smile. So why am I including this dubious place? Because it is one of the more uniquely beautiful hotel renovations I've seen. If the management ever gets its act together and learns how to treat people, this could be one of New York City's very interesting places to stay.

Directly across the street from the Royalton is the Algonquin Hotel. If you're of the opinion that the Algonquin is the epitome of charm and heartwarming nostalgia, then believe me, the Royalton is the essence of high-tech sophistication and drama. You enter through oversized magenta acrylic doors that bring you to a balcony-like hallway that borders the hotel's lounge. Shades of cream and pale lime green cover the avant-garde, high-backed sofas and chairs; the groupings are well spaced and create most unusual settings for romantic conversation. As you continue past the lounge, a small, minimalistic restaurant (at this writing only opened for breakfast and lunch) is at the end of the short marble-clad promenade. But the rooms are the highlight, though you find them through hallways which are too dimly lit and narrow, like a cruise ship's. Once inside, even the standard rooms carry the slick theme to its ultimate conclusion. They have impressive gray and magenta interiors, most with immense bathtubs large enough for bathing *and* dining.

THE STANHOPE HOTEL
995 5th Avenue *at 81st Street*
288-5800
Very, Very Expensive and Beyond

The Stanhope is something to behold. Overflowing in glorious elegance, it is the stuff of dreams and celebrations. From the moment you cross the threshold you will be taken by the meticulous, renovated detailing; the marble floors, Baccarat chandeliers, antique furnishings, stunning four-star dining rooms and the beautiful, flower-quilted king-size beds, most in huge, king-size suites with marble bathrooms.

There is even maid service three times a day and an almost overly attentive staff. Even the hotels with impressive reputations can't hold a candle to what's inside here. Oh well, they do have weekend rates; unfortunately, they are as high as the weekly rates at most other New York hotels. Perhaps this is for one of those splurges that you talk about for years to come.

THE UNITED NATIONS PLAZA HOTEL
One United Nations Plaza *at 44th Street & 1st Avenue*
355-3400
Very, Very Expensive

This is truly a wonderful high-rise hotel. It is directly across the street from the United Nations, which has nothing to do with why it's wonderful or romantic except maybe for the spacious park next to it. The desirability exists in the hotel itself and the neighborhood. First of all, the guest rooms don't begin until the 28th floor, and so regardless of your room number you're guaranteed enviable skyline views of the city and water (an almost priceless commodity in New York hotels). There is a full facility health club on the 27th floor with a window-enclosed full-sized pool, and the rooms are simple but lovely. The area is also one of the quietest in all of Manhattan. The weekend rates are among the most reasonable, around $130 per night or $140 for a deluxe room. During weekdays, the rate is pretty much the same as in the rest of the major Manhattan hotels. If you want to get up and away, but not that far, this might be an indulgence too good to ignore.

> "HE GAVE HER A LOOK YOU COULD HAVE
> SPREAD ON A WAFFLE."
>
> *Ring Lardner*

♦ Restaurant Kissing ♦

Given New York's passion for restaurants, and particularly restaurants with invitingly seductive atmospheres, there was a constant problem of choice when it came to which dining spots should be included in this book. Keep in mind that the last thing we wanted was for this kissing guide to become strictly a dining guide. On the other hand, we'd be crazy to ignore the obvious, and, in New York, romantic dining is definitely the primary way to spend time together.

The problem of separating out the endless possibilities created interesting discussions. We all agreed that a restaurant, to be included, had to have more than opaque lighting, pretty china, intimidating waiters and yards of linen tablecloths. That "more" part was always difficult but the restaurants listed in this section were going to have to have that elusive "more" quality. Diligently we searched through the recommendations of other reviewers, restaurant critics and the New Yorkers we interviewed. Herein we give you a romantic overview of the best kissing restaurants in New York City for all pocketbooks, palates, temperaments and almost all ethnic preferences.

Note: If we missed your favorite romantic restaurant it was probably more due to indigestion than anything else (our hearts were in it, but not our stomachs). The diary section at the back of the book is for your own notes and personal additions to be reviewed at your own pace and when your hearts get hungry.

American Kissing

The Europeans say that Americans aren't romantic, that we know very little about tending to matters of the heart. They think that there is nothing less endearing than eating a hamburger or hot dog and that fast food dining means the death of intimacy. Granted, hamburgers and hot dogs have very little to do with romance and everything to do with baseball or family gatherings, and fast food dining definitely has nothing to do with intimacy, but those aren't the only kind of American restaurants around. In spite of the fact that most of the romantic dining spots we found featured ethnic cuisine, we did find those beautiful places that reflected American style, food and romance.

THE ALGONQUIN'S ROSE ROOM
59 West 44th Street *between 5th & 6th Avenues*
840-6800
Moderate to Expensive

I had heard that the Algonquin was run down and deteriorating, perhaps even tacky. Well, those reviewers must equate charm with high-tech renovations and imposing surroundings. The Algonquin is none of those things, although it is indeed charm personified. Separate from its history, which alone can send any couple who shares a love of literature into a tizzy, The Rose Room is quaint and pretty, closely resembling its past stature as a place to have engaging meals, including a late-night dessert buffet, and talk the hours away. The Algonquin's Oak Room (see Cabaret/Lounge section) is one of the handsomest dining rooms in the city, where the best cabaret singers from all over the world perform. There is nothing even remotely tacky here. It is not the slickest place in the city; yes, the rugs in the main room aren't new and there is a definite feeling of walking back in time to the 40s, but that can be for some a preferable affectionate atmosphere. This nostalgic location is one of a kind and not to be overlooked when you're seeking an all-encompassing, enchanting evening or weekend for two.

AMERICAN FESTIVAL CAFE
30 Rockefeller Center at 50th Street *between 5th and 6th Avenues*
246-6699
Inexpensive to Moderate

Everything about the American Festival Cafe is delightfully and casually romantic, so much so that you can totally ignore its touristy demeanor. The people you are likely to find in here are actually a rare blend of out-of-towners and locals, because it is indeed such an endearing location. During the winter, for breakfast, lunch or dinner, you can sit inside and watch the fabled New York skaters through large wraparound windows take their chances on the ice. You might even fulfill your fantasy and become one of them. In summer, outdoor tables take the place of the slip and slide show, and you can enjoy a leisurely meal sans cars, cabs and street traffic. Coming here always feels like one of the most romantic things to do in New York.

♦ *Romantic Suggestion:* Depending on your body temperature and ability, the restaurant offers skate-a-date, which can prove to be a fabulous evening event for two. Your three-course, prix fixe, well-served meal includes entrance to the rink, skate rental and hot mulled cider served outside. I can't think of a more congenial, affectionate way to spend time.

♦ *Romantic Option:* Savories, 246-6457 (Inexpensive) is a stylish cafeteria just around the circle from the Festival Cafe. Good food and the exact same view are available at much lower prices.

♦ *Second Romantic Option:* Still within the circle that makes up the lower concourse of Rockefeller Center is the **Sea Grill Restaurant, 246-9201** (Expensive). This is the next level up from the less formal Festival Cafe, and it fill its niche respectably. Designed for more exclusive dining, the room is stunning and the menu sophisticated and classic. The same outdoor sights are there to bolster the warm feelings inside. The Sea Grill offers outdoor seating in a romantic garden during the spring and summer. (The restaurant serves only lunch and dinner.)

JEZEBEL'S
630 9th Avenue *at 45th Street*
582-1045
Moderate to Expensive

A lazy, mint-julep, summer afternoon is what you will find inside at Jezebel's any month of the year or any time of the day. The atmosphere is as intoxicating as the fragrant Southern delicacies that will convince your palate, as well as your other senses, that you are no longer in New York City, but somewhere in the deep South. Time takes on a new meaning when you visit here. It's a way of dining and courting that could become *downright regular.*

MARYLOU'S
21 West 9th Street *between 5th & 6th Avenues*
533-0012
Expensive

Down a few steps from this attractive West Village street, just made for leisurely walking, is Marylou's. Inside, past the elegant but merry bar, alive with the sounds of jazz or classical music, is the more sedate restaurant looking very much like the interior of a countryside estate and inspiring soft whispers and lingering conversation. Even when crowded, as it often is, the atmosphere is quiet and relaxed. Pink linens and colorful china decorate the tables. Fresh flowers overflow tastefully from atop antique hutches placed beneath unusual but captivating and individually lit works of art. The fireplaces seem very much at home in two of the four dining rooms and they are always put to good use. From the wood moldings to the old books, a couple could lose track of time while dining on caviar, the freshest seafood, the tenderest meats and vintage wine. Add to that the attentive, cordial service, fringed antique lamps tuned considerately dim and embarrassingly indulgent desserts, and you may forget that there's another couple sitting a bit too close for real *kissing* privacy. (There are a few tables for two that are all by themselves, and if you're lucky enough to be at Marylou's when it's not crowded, you may request them, but they cannot be reserved.)

◆ *Romantic Option:* Marylou's quiet night life is a part of Greenwich Village that is often overshadowed by the frenzied jazz and rock clubs of Bleecker Street, but the slower tempo is there, and it exudes a charm not found elsewhere in the eclectic textures that make up the fabric of this intense neighborhood. To make it linger a little longer, after dinner, walk over to **One Fifth Avenue Bar, 2 East 8th Street, 260-3434** (Moderate), and continue the evening and mood. Don't hurry, this is a piano bar worth spending considerable time in.

ONE if by LAND, TWO if by SEA
17 Barrow Street *at West 4th Street*
255-8649
Very, Very Expensive

As I peered in through the windows I knew that the evening was going to be one I would remember forever. The restaurant seemed to be glowing from two well-stoked fireplaces that enhanced the already scintillating atmosphere. The entrees were almost as attractive as the room and they tasted better than they looked. The waiters were patient and considerate, the surroundings elegant and stately. It was an evening that would make any occasion special. (We wish you a patient cab driver, this is a tricky address to find, though that's an additional kissing advantage.)

R.H. TUGS, Staten Island — See Snug Harbor (Outdoor)

RIVER CAFE

One Water Street, Brooklyn Heights
(718) 522-5200
Expensive

Take the Manhattan Bridge to Brooklyn. Drive one long block to Tillary Street and turn right. When Tillary ends at Cadman Plaza, turn right again. Follow the road which winds around to the right, towards the East River. At the end of the street, the River Cafe is on your right.

Friends gave us a wedding present of brunch at the River Cafe, and in every way, it was a gift to savor. The food was creatively prepared, very good and caringly served. But the real gift was the thrilling view looking out from the glass-enclosed dining room. Renovated in the mid-'70s, the River Cafe is an enormous white barge with an enormous, crystal clear glass wall facing west. A few portholes remain as authentic touches of the past. Towering, glorious flower arrangements brighten the dining room and cocktail lounge. Sitting closely together, gaze out at the Statue of Liberty, South Street Seaport, the lower Manhattan skyline and the stonework of the Brooklyn Bridge. Watch the river traffic, as the color of the water changes in sync with the movement of the sun across the sky.

Note: Come for a drink at sunset, for lunch or dinner, or brunch on weekends. Waterside tables outside are coveted in the summer. Jackets required after 6 p.m. This is a popular place, so make reservations. If you're coming for drinks: As you may have guessed, the bar gets crowded around sunset.

◆ *Romantic Option:* Just south of the River Cafe on Fulton Ferry Landing is **Bargemusic (718) 624-4061**, a uniquely romantic concert site. Talented musicians perform *"Chamber Music with a Different View"* brilliantly on Thursdays at 7:30 and Sundays at 4 p.m. Another renovated barge, this one sways to the harmonies of the music, or is it the flow of the river? Rows of folding seats face the performers against a majestic skyline backdrop. Go topside on the double-decker former coffee barge for preconcert conversation or intermission. Dress is casual, thank goodness, and the prices are very reasonable. (Reservations are needed.)

◆ *Second Romantic Option:* While in **Brooklyn Heights**, wander along **The Promenade**, three blocks south of historic Fulton Ferry Landing. With its moving views and many benches, it's a perfect spot for a walk or a sunset. On nice sunny days, it's full of runners, bikers, small children, families and other couples like yourselves.

RUMPELMAYERS
50 Central Park South *at 59th Street*
755-5800
Inexpensive

There are going to be more than a few locals who are going to disagree with this entry, but we voted, and this overly pink, Central Park, somewhat out-of-date ice cream parlor won its recognition as a place to enjoy old-fashioned romance, which, when you think about it, is hard to come by these days. There was a time when a sundae wasn't a designer escapade with elite-sounding names and price tags. There was a time when a boy would take a girl to the local ice cream shoppe and they would share whatever gooey offering they could handle. Well, indeed, times have changed, but the chance to relive a more innocent way of life is an opportunity not to be overlooked. And, yes, the interior is pink and during the summer or weekends grandma may be taking junior out for a sugar rush, but at the off hours, after a morning hansom cab ride through the park or an afternoon playful romp through F.A.O. Schwarz (see Miscellaneous Kissing), a very serious sundae, with a few discreetly placed kisses in between licks, at Rumpelmayers, should just about make the day as joyous as they come.

Brunch/Breakfast Kissing

I am always searching for the quintessential romantic breakfast. The kind of place where mornings succumb to the heart's longing for time to pass slowly with nothing to do but sip another cafe au lait and find solace in prolonging sunrise another hour or two. Whether it be Sunday or during the week, that dreamy awakening is possible and enjoyable at several huggable, eye-opening places in and around town. If you can find your way out of bed before 11 on Sunday, most of these places will not even have a waiting line. Many of these morning kissing spots are not even vaguely known for the infamous New York power breakfasts. On the rare occasion when you find one in progress, be assured that, for the most part, it is the exception to the rule. (Note: Some places are only opened for brunch on weekends, others offer both brunch and breakfast.)

BERRY'S
180 Spring Street *at Thompson Street*
226-4394
Inexpensive to Moderate

Weekend brunch is only a large part of what this lovingly intimate, reasonably priced restaurant does best. Particularly on Saturdays, when the Sunday brunch crowd is out shopping and running errands. This place also comes with an emphatic warning: Berry's can get crowded, noisy, very smoky and, because it is so intimate, unpleasant. Until the management institutes a no-smoking policy, go there cautiously or cross the street to the **Manhattan Cafe, 129 Spring Street, 966-3459** (Moderate), where the size and atmosphere and great food can make the morning a beautiful affair.

THE BLUE HEN
88 7th Avenue *between 15th & 16th Streets*
645-3015
Inexpensive

This is classic country brunching at its best, a haven from anything even vaguely connected with city life, except the occasional *New York Times* being read by a news-hungry couple. The room is quaint, done in hues of blue and pink, and the food is fabulous, a total heartwarming surprise.

CAFE des ARTISTES
1 West 67th Street *at Central Park West*
877-3500
Moderate (for brunch only)

The countryside has moved indoors at Cafe des Artistes and the environment couldn't be more inviting. Well-tended greenery is everywhere and the cheerful room is provocatively lit. The breakfast is Continental food at its best, and the presentation, like the interior, will please your senses. This place is probably too popular to be a truly romantic spot, but we so thoroughly enjoyed our Sunday brunch here that I had to include it. (Very well known and luscious Continental menu for lunch and dinner too.)

PARIS COMMUNE
411 Bleecker *between 10th & 11th Streets*
929-0509
Inexpensive

This modest restaurant, with its small array of wood tables, oil paintings and rustic, casual ambience exudes a Parisian Left Bank atmosphere. Weekend brunch is fresh and beautifully served. It's a shame they serve only dinner during the week.

THE PEMBROKE ROOM — See The Lowell Hotel (Hotel Kissing)

SARABETH'S KITCHEN
412 Amsterdam Avenue *between 80th & 81st Streets*
496-6280
1295 Madison Avenue *between 92nd & 93rd Streets*
410-7335
Both are Inexpensive

I think it is very considerate of Sarabeth to give us two of the most romantically perfect locations to have breakfast with a choice between the East and West Sides. Our preference is the East Side with its tall jade-green french windows and french door entranceway. The menu is wonderful, with eggs, granola and fresh-baked goods. The East Side has a balcony section that helps separate the two dining areas — a definite yes when it comes to crowded (note: very-long-lines crowded) Sundays. Both restaurants are bright and cheery and practically empty on weekday mornings.

SUMMERHOUSE
50 East 86th Street *at Madison Avenue*
249-6300
Inexpensive

The omelet was fluffy and with it was served a fresh, sweet strawberry butter with warm melt-in-your mouth biscuits by somewhat distracted (it can be busy), though polite, waitpeople. (Theirs is one interesting brunch menu, they even serve a Huevos Rancheros Pizza.) The cafe-styled interior is simple and classic, with a warm, casual atmosphere — perhaps a little on the crowded side to be a quiet spot for two over brunch and Sunday morning conversation, but be patient, once you're at your own table for two, it is possible that you won't notice anyone else except each other.

Cafe Kissing

There comes a time in every romantic involvement when two people look deep into each other's eyes and say: *"Let us eat cake and anything else sugary we can get our hands on."* At other times, when your beloved is obviously in need of a long talk, the informed romantic will suggest that the mood be supported by a well-brewed espresso or calmed by herbal tea and enriched by something sweetly decadent. Sometimes romance requires the old-world grace and pace that only a cafe can provide. For such times and needs, consult the following tastefully and sincerely compiled compendium. (Note: Because the typical fare at most cafes is light, all of them listed here are rated inexpensive.)

CAFE BORGIA
185 Bleecker Street *at MacDougal Street*
473-2290

Cafe Borgia is a Village landmark that has been tempting lovers with plates of little delicious cookies for years. On a beautiful spring day, its outdoor table can't be beat.

CAFE de CORTINA
1448 2nd Avenue *between 75th & 76th Streets*
517-2066

Simply lovely. One of the most affectionate places to partake of everything from Belgian waffles to crepes, desserts and a perfect cappuccino, which is an emotional experience in and of itself. With the person you love sharing it all, it can be heaven.

CAFE SHA SHA
510 Hudson Street *at Charles Street*
242-3021

Cafe Sha Sha has two things that make it a good kissing place: it's
in the far-West Village and it's very quiet. Technically it's too big
for a cafe, but this allows for space between one romance and the next.

CAFFE LUCCA
228 Bleecker Street *at Cornelia Street*
243-8385

Here's a place in which you'll want to linger. It has a few tables
for dining alfresco which are occupied into the wee hours in the warm
months. The cozy interior is a rendezvous for a serious — and seriously
romantic — cafe crowd. By the way, if you ask them when they open
and close, they'll say, *"Till late."*

CAFFE REGGIO
119 MacDougal Street *at Prince Street*
475-9557

The most authentic-looking of the cafes in New York with its
jumble of marble tables and imposing coffee urns and samovars, Caffe
Reggio will make you think you're in the old country, where time
slows down and moods turn softer. At times it does suffer from the
tourist trade, but if you want the look and feel of a real cafe, this is
it. Going during off hours, however, is the best option here, as in
most New York cafes (or caffes if Italian is your preference).

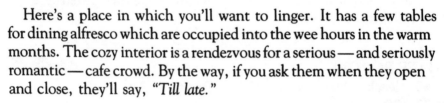

CAFFE VIVALDI
32 Jones Street *at 7th Avenue South*
691-7538

Both this street and, as a result, this caffe, are hard to find (for you and everyone else) so you should have more quiet moments here. The fireplace in winter will also keep the two of you warm and glowing. You can also enjoy some of the best and freshest pastries around, and the interior will be peaceful and warm while you're eating.

CLOISTER STREET CAFE
29 Cornelia Street *at Bleecker Street*
989-9319

A little bit of everything a cafe lover could want is waiting at this gem of a coffee house — outdoor seating in summer, a fireplace in winter, poetry and prose on Sundays, and a relaxing, laid-back, easy atmosphere. Life together should always be like this.

DANAL
90 East 10th Street *at 3rd Avenue*
982-6930

Ah, the aroma, the setting, the warm service — everything you need except a favorite other to share it with. This may be one of the most enchanting places in the Village. Danal even has a tucked away garden for outdoor seating in the warmer months.

De ROBERTIS
176 1st Avenue *at 12th Street*
674-7137

A truly wonderful, handsome, period piece of an Italian caffe brightly lit with lots of privacy. The pastries can be too sweet — even for the sweet — but two forks and one dessert can go a long way here.

GRAN CAFFE degli ARTISTI
46 Greenwich Avenue *between 9th & West 10th Streets*
255-7041

They say there's no love like an eternal love and this venerable caffe has played host to couples for years. The lone cappuccino maven might even feel out of place here — it is that much the province of old loves, new loves and soon-to-be loves. The several rooms of Gran Caffe degli (say *DALE-yee* if you want to sound like a native) Artisti serve as a variety of hide-outs for those in search of a quiet time, a delicious cake or cannoli and perhaps a strong coffee. Your privacy increases as you venture farther into the caffe; beyond the two front rooms, there is a smaller room in the back, and beyond this, one very small room with only two tables. Although nothing could surpass these candlelit rooms for a warm finish to a fall or winter afternoon or evening, they're also great for cooling off in the warmer months with a lemonade or sparkling house-special drink. And if you're not in the mood for dark woody surroundings, a seat by the picture window, on the parlor floor up front, lets you eye the passing scene without being observed.

♦ *Romantic Warning:* Many true loves have gone astray trying to find this somewhat secluded spot. Since it's up off the street, be sure to remember the exact house number.

♦ *Romantic Option:* Since the Gran Caffe never loses a customer, it can be crowded on weekend evenings. If you're in that cafe mood, continue down Greenwich Avenue to the **Peacock Caffe, 24 Greenwich, 242-9395** (Inexpensive), another delicious spot. It is a tranquil, nostalgic, quite Italian place with lovely classical music playing in the background. Always romantic.

HUNGARIAN PASTRY SHOP
1030 Amsterdam Avenue *at 111th Street*
866-4230

Pleasantly off the beaten track and almost too pleasantly satisfying for anyone's diet. Primarily frequented by Columbia University students, this pastry shop will surely have something to take care of the gypsy in your souls. And you'd swear through the smoke — the only place in the world where smoke is required for atmosphere — that Jack Kerouac was having a chat with Allen Ginsberg.

LANCIANI PATISSERIE
275 West 4th Street *at West 11th Avenue*
929-0739

A handsome, sparkling room served by a caring staff and patronized by an elegant clientele. An exuberant place at heart, it may be too quick-pulsed for some but off hours will prove calm and tranquil and very rich.

RUMBULS PASTRY SHOP
20 Christopher Street *at 7th Avenue South*
924-8900

A quiet cafe whose small, warm, wood-paneled rooms take the cake (sorry) for beautiful decoration and heartwarming ambience. Their selection is creamy and temptingly presented.

Chinese Kissing

For some reason I have never found Chinese restaurants a refuge for affectionate interacting. Perhaps it's because the best way to eat Chinese cuisine is in a large group where you get to taste more than just what you order. The endless variety of meat and fish dishes with a unique melange of vegetables makes eating with less than three feel like you're being cheated, which sums up to being tasty but not romantic. But then again, this is New York, and the lack of chopsticks for two has been handled quite nicely by a few restaurants that have turned the lights down low, softened the pace and created just the right blend of ambience and excellent cuisine to delight even the most finicky of chop suey lovers.

AUNTIE YUAN
1191 1st Avenue *at 64th Street*
744-4040
Expensive

Auntie Yuan borders on too popular because it happens to be one of the best Uptown Chinese restaurants around, but it feels appropriately romantic in spite of all that. Auntie's (we're on intimate terms) is for when you're in the mood for high style that still radiates some amount of desirable coziness with exotic food to match.

CHEZ VONG
220 East 46th *at 3rd Avenue*
867-1111
Expensive

From the moment we entered this hallowed, very elaborately decorated restaurant we knew that something special waited for us. Everything was set for sumptuous dining from the traditional, dramatic Chinese decor to the extensive (actually, "extensive" is an understatement), well-served menu.

PEARL'S
38 West 48th Street *between 5th & 6th Avenues*
221-6677
Expensive

This striking room brings elegance to Chinese dining, and the gracious staff makes you feel that your meal is something more than special. Even lunch will feel more like an event than a mere dining escape. The sleek, sophisticated inside is a welcome change of pace in a wonderful setting.

SHUN LEE
43 West 65th Street *near Columbus Avenue*
595-8895
Expensive

Shun Lee is one sexy Chinese restaurant. The setting is a mysterious mixture of blacks with dramatic spotlights poised over each table. The menu is far from mysterious, it is blatantly delicious. Any couple will find the experience here worthy of a special occasion.

SHUN LEE PALACE
155 East 55th Street *between Lexington & 3rd Avenues*
371-8844
Expensive

Everything about this Shun Lee is designed to be impressive. It is a truly posh, truly popular location with a truly excellent menu that makes dining here truly wonderful. When you find yourselves in a need for Chinese food, this place can tend to everything very nicely.

Continental Kissing

There is something very *de rigueur* about this style of dining. It encompasses the best of most every cuisine there is, served in an atmosphere that feels very elegant and very European with the emphasis leaning heavily toward French and Italian dishes. For amorous couples with eclectic appetites there is nothing quite as satisfying as Continental dining — particularly here in New York City, where the chefs are some of the best in the world.

THE AMBASSADOR BAR and GRILL
One United Nations Plaza *at 44th Street & 1st Avenue*
702-5014
Moderate

Give me elegance, good food and reasonable prices any day and I can feel as loving and adoring as the most die-hard romantic you know. The Ambassador Bar and Grill provides just such an atmosphere, and it is secluded, in an out-of-the-mainstream quiet neighborhood. The emphasis inside is leisurely, complemented by a soothing atmosphere, plus the prix fixe lunch or dinner is relatively reasonable and extremely satisfying.

You enter this spacious restaurant through a glass-ceilinged entryway, designed to resemble a contemporary greenhouse, which brings you to a large reception alcove that is totally separate from the dining room and bar. This entryway prevents you from feeling that you've intruded on someone else's intimate tête-à-tête when you arrive. The dramatic scarlet rug throughout is offset by another atrium-styled skylight in the main room, and the glass-paneled walls add an additional light-and-airy feeling all around. After savoring a delectable four-course meal you can retire into the lounge offering background music (that stays in the background), and cocktails or espresso. This one spot can make for an all-encompassing interlude for two, after dark, in New York.

CAFE des ARTISTES — See Restaurants Brunch/Breakfast

THE CARLYLE RESTAURANT and CAFE
Madison Avenue *at 76th Street*
744-1600
Very, Very Expensive

I'm usually skeptical when I hear about well-known, luxuriant hotel dining rooms being truly intimate. Most are too stuffy, too business-oriented or they take themselves much too seriously for the tender needs of snuggling and affection. The Carlyle is, in all honesty, a little, and at times a great deal, of all those things and can prove to be a tiresome, pretentious burden, especially when all it takes is for the staff to lighten up. But it is also Uptown New York at its best, with all the right touches and all the right details to make any time of day seem special and intimate. The interior is impeccable. The food is extraordinary. There's a profusion of flowers everywhere, and one can go for breakfast, lunch, dinner, brunch, teatime and/or cocktails. At night there's even the eternal Bobby Short playing Cole Porter tunes in the Cafe Carlyle. For a thoroughly *suave* time of it, come here, concentrate on each other and enjoy a memorable dining experience.

540 PARK
540 Park Avenue *at 61st Street*
759-4100
Very, Very Expensive and Beyond

If dining in a French country chateau on a scale only slightly less majestic than Versailles is to your taste, then this location is prime territory for just that, with a menu that is simple, classic and enticing. The only warning this exquisite setting carries is its deserved reputation as the place for *"power eating,"* which can create awkward vibes when the mood you want is warm and endearing. Let's hope that *"gentle romancing"* is not the wave of the future.

GARVIN'S
19 Waverly Place *7th Avenue South at Greenwich Street*
474-5261
Moderate to Expensive

   Garvin's is a poetic city nightspot, right in the middle of what is
not the most poetic part of the Village. The restaurant's motif is
reminiscent of the 1900s with a Victorian flare. The walls are covered
with oversized mirrors and tapestries, the elegant table settings are
arranged to facilitate close encounters and vases filled with a profusion
of flowers adorn antiques throughout the room. Overhead the
spotlighting is all in pink, which makes the interior even more
romantic than this provincial, downtown setting creates on its own.
The Continental menu is a worthy complement to the ambience.
Now you only need a companion to share it with, and the evening
or afternoon is complete.
   ◆ ***Romantic Suggestion:*** **Cafe Lido,** next door to Garvin's,
533-4151, is a lovely, unusually spacious jazz club intimately related
to Garvin's. It shares much of the same intriguing decor and lighting,
plus some of the best new music in the city. There is no cover and
no minimum most evenings. This place can make for one smooth,
kissable night out.

GOTHAM BAR & GRILL
12 East 12th Street *between 5th & University Place*
620-4020
Expensive to Very Expensive

   The Gotham Bar & Grill is a beautiful three, and sometimes four,
star restaurant. Perhaps a bit too much on the formal side for some
affectionate tastes, but the sparkling elegance down here in the
Village has never looked so good. Holding hands over a serious,
well-paced dinner here can be an all-night affair; or appetizers alone
can serve as a welcoming introduction for things to come. From the
street the tall windows reveal only a suggestion as to the striking
eccentric interior. Scads of muslin material float like parachutes from

the overhead fixtures, diffusing the lighting throughout the restaurant. The dining room itself borders on enormous, which for you is a kissing advantage. No one feels encumbered at this restaurant. Beautiful tones of green and rose are accented by floor-to-ceiling french windows (probably 30 or 40 feet tall), and the tables are softly lit to give a vibrant glow to each setting. You can take this one to heart.

GREGORY'S, Bronx — See Bronx River Parkway Path (Outdoor)

NIGHTFALLS
7612 Third Avenue, Brooklyn
(718) 748-8703
Moderate to Expensive

Take the Brooklyn Bridge to the Brooklyn-Queens Expressway (278) west. Follow the Belt Parkway east to Exit 1 (67th Street). Bear right until the traffic light. Staying right, go up 67th Street one block to 3rd Avenue and turn right. Nightfalls is ten blocks ahead on your right.

As a new, reluctantly transplanted Manhattanite, I was dubious when my husband suggested a bike ride to deepest Brooklyn. *"I think I can show you some things you'll like,"* he promised. He was joking, right? Brooklyn romantic? I wasn't born yesterday! Cajoled into giving it a try, I pedaled along to Bay Ridge with him, where he stopped somewhere on 3rd Avenue. I looked in amazement at Nightfalls. We went inside. It was tasteful, sophisticated and beautiful. The edges of my resistance to outer-borough life began to melt away.

Nightfalls is different; subtly dramatic. Generous floral arrangements are placed everywhere. Arches and columns create lots of separate spaces so that you have a modest feeling of seclusion. At the rear of the two-story restaurant is its namesake: a very high cascade of water spilling down a garden wall. In front of the falls, trees are strewn with lights. In nice weather, you can sit outside beside the water. In winter the view from indoors is also worth a visit. Its glass-atrium exterior puts you right next to the waterfall. Ask for a window table, although with all that glass, you won't miss the view from any spot. Oh, and the food: the Continental fare is artfully prepared and served. Ultra-rich desserts are a specialty: try the bittersweet chocolate mousse in an almond tulip with fresh raspberry sauce. After dinner, try the second floor bar, where there is often live music.

♦ **Romantic Warning:** Outdoor seating, glorious in spring, can be too hot in warm weather. It also gets crowded on weekends, which makes reservations essential.

♦ **Romantic Option:** The Greenhouse Cafe, 7717 3rd Avenue, **Brooklyn, (718) 833-8200** (Moderate), is a relaxed, affable place for brunch; **Areo's, 8420 3rd Avenue, Brooklyn, (718) 238-0079** (Inexpensive), is a romantic cafe for Italian fare; and **Once Upon a Sundae, 7702 3rd Avenue, Brooklyn, (718) 748-3412** (Inexpensive), is an adorable place for something creamy and lusciously covered with chocolate or fudge. These eateries are all within walking distance of each other on the very yuppified, very strollable 3rd Avenue.

RAINBOW ROOM
30 Rockefeller Center *on the 65th Floor*
632-5000
Very, Very Expensive

If I was told once, I was told a hundred times that I could not finish this book without including an evening of dinner and dancing at the Rainbow Room. There was no other single place in the entire city that received such enthusiastic, consistent romantic praise. That alone made me skeptical, but far be it from me to argue without firsthand information.

Well, for the most part I do see why almost anyone would consider this room exceedingly romantic. The setting is striking. When you enter you will instantly feel as if you are dancing on top of the world with your special date some time back in the '30s or '40s. Three tiers of tables surround a revolving dance floor with two-story windows revealing an absolutely stunning view of the twinkling city beyond.

The food is notable and the service graceful and considerate. And the music — a twelve-piece orchestra that plays music the way it was meant to be performed. A two-step into the past couldn't be more beguiling than this . . . except for the price, which is as far removed from the '30s as you can get. It would not be surprising if your evening totaled $100 or more per person. Those people who thought this was an unquestionably romantic must are probably on an expense account.

Note: Dancing and dinner go together, which explains the hefty price tag on this evening out. Although if you dine after 10:30, the light supper menu is served and the cost can drop to almost half.

◆ *Romantic Option:* If you can't dance or your budget doesn't permit, the **Rainbow Promenade,** adjacent to the Rainbow Room, is a wonderful, much less expensive alternative with the same view, a charming romantic interior and the same kitchen preparing very good *lighter* fare. The piano music is simpler than the sounds next door, but it is entertaining nevertheless and a perfect background to the conversation at hand.

SIGN of the DOVE
1110 Third Avenue *at 65th Street*
861-8080
Very Expensive

By reputation this is among the ultimate in romantic dining. Ask just about any savvy New Yorker to list the city's best spots for intimate dining and you'll hear this name — even if the New Yorker hasn't eaten here. It is a very stunning dining room. The food is fabulous, the piano music subtle and melodic and the rose-tinted walls and candlelit, flower bedecked room provocative. Sign of the Dove fits perfectly into this book.

THE SUMPTUARY RESTAURANT
400 Third Avenue *between 28th & 29th Streets*
889-6056
Moderate

"Oh no," I thought last night as my friends and I stumbled into this enchanting, whimsical, offbeat dining establishment, *"not another restaurant for the book."* *"Oh yes,"* my own voice countered. I must have stepped out of New York and into *Alice in Wonderland.* Stop the presses, it would be a disservice not to include such a phantasmagorical eating experience as this, with its fine service, quiet flute and violin melodies, pink table linens, the room strewn with little white lights, strangely flickering fireplaces, bird ornaments, paintings, bas-reliefs everywhere and little funny touches that would seem out of place anywhere else (is that a little green mask that bird on the wall is wearing?). I'm telling you, there's a profound magic at the sumptuous Sumptuary Restaurant.

The food, described on one of the many unusual window signs outside as eclectic, is characterized by the same offbeat charm as the atmosphere (how does Apricot and Plum Duckling grab you, for example?). Our meal was delightful and far less expensive than most comparable meals around town.

Note: There are two floors; don't miss touring them both. You'll also notice that there's a small garden in back where meals are served on warm days. It was closed on my last visit, but I for one can't wait to go back when it's open.

THE TERRACE RESTAURANT
400 West 119th Street *at Morningside Drive*
666-9490
Very Expensive

It's the little touches that make the Terrace such a special place to visit. Perhaps it's the azaleas blooming in the entryway where your coats are checked or the live harp music that is piped through the restaurant at just the right decibel level that brings me back to this hidden jewel time and time again. Or maybe the real enticement is the single rose in a crystal vase that sits atop each table or the slim candle that is replaced by the ever-attentive staff before it burns too low. Whatever it is for you, the understated refinement of the Terrace, the dazzling view from its 17th-floor windows and the nearly perfect cuisine draw a dedicated following night after night. Squirreled away in a Columbia University-owned building, the Terrace is a favorite splurge for a romantic tête-á-tête. Be warned that you won't get away cheaply, although we did avoid the beluga caviar appetizer ($65) in favor of warm goat's cheese salad ($9.50) and settled for a lovely bottle of fume blanc ($25) instead of the 1975 Chateau Petrus ($500). But once you decide to make this the place for your personal celebration, let yourselves go and enjoy it. By the way, there really is a terrace at the Terrace, so be certain to step outside for a moment after you've eaten and admire the extraordinary skyline of a most extraordinary city.

THE WATER'S EDGE, Queens — See Long Island City Waterfront (Outdoor)

French Kissing

The obvious pun is even too much for me, so please forgive the momentary cheap indulgence — this is not the section for those with athletic tongues — this is the section for true food lovers who feel that their relationship is best reflected in their joint belief that a succulent coq au vin or coquilles St. Jacques is the perfect prelude to amour. For those in search of tantalizing the palate as well as the heart, here are our suggestions for places in which to appreciate the pleasures of a truly smooth, complex sauce; a wicked combination of textures and flavors; the ecstasy of art-worthy presentations all served

on the most translucent select china — all dedicated to creating
rapturous dining for two.

AU TROQUET
328 West 12th *between Hudson & Washington Streets*
924-3413
Expensive

An inviting room, delectable food, and for this caliber of dining,
reasonable prices — those are things that can encourage caring
feelings any night of the week.

THE BOX TREE RESTAURANT — See The Box Tree Hotel
(Hotel/Lodging)

BRIVE
405 East 58th *between 1st & 2nd Avenues*
838-9393
Expensive

Truly one of the more beautiful settings, with everything an
evening out should supply: superb food, enchanting, classic French
decor, courteous service and all the time you need to capture every
moment and savor it. *One of the best!*

CAFE du PARC
106 East 19th Street *between Park Avenue and Irving Place*
777-7840
Expensive

Intimate French dining in this extremely pretty location is a must
for any discussion that requires good food, truly charming decor and
courteous, intelligent service.

CAFE EUROPA & LA BRIOCHE
347 East 54th *between 2nd & 3rd Avenues*
755-0160
Moderate to Expensive

My managing editor insisted we go here, declaring this to be one of her favorite romantic spots in New York. While we were dining, she kept pointing to the details around the room to make sure I wouldn't forget anything. She wanted me to capture the mood just right. *"Describe the tapestry and the hand-carved oak woodwork,"* she insisted. *"Notice how the room is beautifully quaint and very European with only a hint of contemporary touches. It's petite but not crowded. The lighting is soft and bright instead of somber and dark like so many other places."* Emphatically she added, *"This setting could easily be Brussels or Switzerland. And remember to explain how during the holidays the decorations are so special and heartwarming."* With that, the gentleman next to us, who apologized for eavesdropping, asked if he could add his feelings to the discussion. In a thick Southern-drawl he said that he agreed with everything but hoped I wouldn't forget to mention how perfect a spot this can be in the spring. *"It actually makes New York feel fresh and relaxed when you're finished eating."* Well, I guess that says it all, except for my two cents, but I agree wholeheartedly. Except I'd like to add that the food and desserts satisfyingly speak for themselves.

CHANTERELLE
89 Grand Street *at Greene Street*
966-6960
Very, Very Expensive

With a handful of tables in an outrageously precious setting Chanterelle serves a gourmet selection of exquisitely prepared creations of French and Continental delights. Given the almost-impossible-to-obtain reservations, careful planning is required for a celebration dining event.

LA GAULOISE

502 6th Avenue *near West 13th Street*
691-1363
Expensive to Very Expensive

My favorite French restaurant, though it is often the agony and
ecstasy when I've taken someone special here to dine or brunch. The
food is exceptional, brunch is a heavenly fare, the interior is a stately
combination of dark wood paneling, art deco sconces and well-placed
mirrors; you will be impressed from the moment you enter. My
hesitation: sometimes the service is haughty, sometimes the room
can be a bit noisy and crowded, and I always spend more money than
I had hoped. Oh well, such is the price of love.

LA TULIPE

104 West 13th Street *between 6th & 7th Avenues*
691-8860
Very, Very Expensive

Though I hate to use the word pretty, this place is just that and
lovingly so. The food is some of the best French cuisine served
anywhere in the world. This one is not for just any romantic
encounter, but for someone truly special.

LE REGENCE — See Hotel Plaza Athenee (Hotel/Lodging)

LUTECE

249 East 50th Street *at 2nd Avenue*
752-2225
Very, Very Expensive

All of the restaurant reviewers in the world who have dined at this
bastion of culinary excellence rate this as one of the best restaurants
in the universe. A gastronomic feat of excellence such as this spot
offers may very well prove to be a richly tantalizing romantic affair.

MAXIM'S — See L'Omnibus (Cabaret/Lounge)

NICOLE BRASSERIE de PARIS
870 7th Avenue *at 56th Street*
765-5108
Moderate to Expensive

This is a lovely French dining experience. It is simply done, without pretense or frills. A few steps down from street level, this window-enclosed dining room offers a soft cafe-like atmosphere with an elegant touch that is comfortable and, in a New York sort of way, romantic.

PETROSSIAN RESTAURANT
182 West 58th Street *at 7th Avenue*
245-2214
Very Expensive

It is hardly a secret that the Petrossian room is an outrageously ritzy place to dine, but I'm not sure it is as well known how wickedly romantic it can be as well. Besides the fact that there is something very New York about eating here (although eating here isn't eating, it's really experiencing), there are two things you must be aware of before you indulge your shared fantasy of caviar and bubbly. First, the management's philosophy is as follows: *"Caviar is not food, it is a dream, a philosophy of life and living,"* and, *"The only thing to serve with good caviar is more caviar,"* and second, they take this belief seriously. From the fluted champagne glasses and the black-and-white-patterned Limoges china on every table that sparkles from the glow of an exquisite antique crystal chandelier overhead, to the staff that is well versed in gourmet delights, this can be intense French dining at its best.

◆ ***Romantic Alternative:*** Though it lacks the finesse and grandeur of the Petrossian Restaurant, the **Caviarteria, 29 East 60th Street, 759-7410,** is always a possibility. Go shopping here for your own supply and create your atmosphere at home or on an outdoor picnic.

The Petrossian has its own take-out area, but I assure you once you're there, you'll want to stay put.

VANESSA'S
289 Bleecker *at 7th Avenue*
243-4225
Expensive to Very Expensive

We visited this place on the insistence of a friend who said the book would be incomplete without Vanessa's, and he was right. This is an invitingly elegant French restaurant, with space for privacy and attention to detail that is welcome and never intrusive. It was a warm, windy Sunday evening when we went (a double date with dear loving friends) and everyone found this country Victorian dining room exceedingly romantic and the food absolutely delicious. All of us expressed our praise of the food and the delightful service in harmonious oohs and aahs after each course. And that was before we knew of the decadently rich desserts ahead. I should also mention that testing out this kind of research in pairs can produce as many giggles as it does kisses, but at Vanessa's we never felt out of place. Elegant romance and stiff shoulders do not have to go hand in hand.

Indian Kissing

There is something mysterious and exotic about Indian cuisine. No matter where I've indulged my longing for tandoori, chapati and lassi, I've always enjoyed the scents, sights, sounds and samplings that are unique to this style of cooking. In addition to the intriguing menu, there also seems to be a reverent quality about the way the waiters handle themselves, you and the food. The gallant service is a trademark to the entire dining ceremony. In thinking about what, if any, of this lends itself to an intimate exchange over dinner, I conclude that it is probably the food as much as the respectful flourish bestowed upon every eating occasion.

AKBAR
256 East 49th Street *at 2nd Avenue*
755-9100
Moderate to Expensive

475 Park Avenue *between 57th & 58th Streets*
838-1717
Expensive

Both of these locations are as pretty as they are elegant. If your taste buds long for exotic spices in a classic New York environment, you will feel delighted with either of these locations. Although the Park Avenue one has beautiful stained glass ceilings, I prefer the food at the 2nd Avenue Akbar.

BUKHARA
148 East 48th Street *between 6th and 7th Avenues*
838-1811
Moderate to Expensive

One of the most handsome and comfortable Indian restaurants in town. The solid, regal decor makes this the romantic's choice for a traditional Indian repast, but the formality ends with the setting. This is a robust eating experience. The tasty lamb and chicken dishes are meant to be eaten with your hands, but don't be concerned, hot towels are brought to your table before you start.

DARBAR
44 West 56th Street *at Madison Avenue*
432-7227
Moderate

This is one of my favorites, and when I remind my husband (whose palate runs to what I refer to as bland and he refers to as basic) that the flavors here are mixed with finesse, and intimate seating is guaranteed, he almost always gives in, because the evening is always as supreme as the food. The waiters are especially caring and attentive, with several assigned to each table.

MADRAS WOODLANDS — See Restaurants Kosher

NIRVANA
30 Central Park South *near 5th Avenue*
486-5700
Moderate to Expensive

Sometimes where an affectionate evening is at stake, a dramatic stroke may be what's required. One of the most dramatic settings for this style cuisine is Nirvana. The view is what lends magic to the already magical (perhaps overdone, perhaps a bit too small but magical nonetheless) interior. The rooftop setting, with an unobstructed view of the park, is enthralling. Everything seems to sparkle peacefully up here — even the food.

PASSAGE TO INDIA
308 East 6th Street *between 1st & 2nd Avenues*
529-5770
Moderate

Cozy is the word for this location, and among a handful of other Indian restaurants in this vicinity, that is quite a compliment and a romantic advantage. Besides the truly tempting selections that include tandoori and marvelous vegetarian creations, the candlelit tables lend an ethereal glow to the meal. This establishment will satisfy your requirements for a sentimental evening, even if your tastes run toward the exotic.

Italian Kissing

I don't know about you, but to me almost anything Italian is lusciously romantic. From art, clothes, movie stars, sculpture, architecture and design to pasta, there is something profoundly arousing about everything reminiscent of this country. And if the food is only a small way of participating, then for me, al dente can become a way of life. Even if you are not engrossed by the culture, the food itself is tantalizing enough to be a worthy enhancement to any evening.

ABBRACCIAMENTO ON THE PIER
2200 Rockaway Parkway, Brooklyn
(718) 251-5517
Moderate to Expensive

From Manhattan, take the Brooklyn Bridge to the Brooklyn-Queens Expressway West. Follow the Belt Parkway East to Exit 13 (Rockaway Parkway). Abbracciamento is just south of the Parkway, on the Canarsie Pier.

As you drive toward Abbracciamento, an array of twinkling lights begins to glitter across the bay. It's hard to believe a place this lovely could exist way out here in Canarsie. *"It's a mini Windows on the World!"* exclaimed my companion once we entered this charming, out-of-the-way establishment and saw the city sparkling in the distance. Go for a romantic dinner on a warm evening. The generous wooden deck on Jamaica Bay has wrought-iron tables with a wonderful vista of sailboats, sea and sky. Views are great from indoors, too, because all of the walls are made of glass. Even in winter, the semicircular restaurant, aglow with candles, is inviting. Spend an evening drifting to a deft piano player's romantic tunes.

◆ **Romantic Option:** Come by boat. Slips are available for customers.

◆ **Romantic Warning:** As with most places, it gets crowded on weekends and reservations become necessary.

ARCOBALENO
21 East 9th Street *at Broadway*
473-2215
Moderate

Take a walk through the Village till you find yourselves at Arcobaleno. The steps will take you down into a wood-tabled country setting with tall framed windows that look out onto a garden veranda in the back. If you're in the neighborhood, walking along the street hand in hand, and the urge for pasta comes over you, indulge that craving here.

CARMELLA'S VILLAGE GARDEN
49 Charles Street *at 7th Avenue South*
242-2155
Very Inexpensive

Carmella's is one of our favorite spots in the city. If you see a couple with a bottle of wine speeding through the village, you can bet they're headed here. The cluster of rooms is dark and handsome in winter, but from spring to late autumn, you must dine under the vines and awnings in the garden. This is one of the least expensive places in New York, but it is so endearing that all lifestyles merge at this location.

CARPACCIO
227 East 50th Street *between 2nd & 3rd Avenues*
838-7808
Expensive

One of the more elegant ways to enjoy Northern Italian fare in New York is to walk down into this stunningly renovated brownstone restaurant and twirl your fork around unequaled pasta and veal creations. And it is definitely romantic.

CHELSEA PLACE
147 Eighth Avenue *between 18th & 19th Streets*
924-8413
Moderate

The setting of Chelsea Place exudes romantic vibrations. Its facade is an antique store which showcases an armoire on the rear wall that is a secret opening to the restaurant. The first room you see is a bar with loud live pop music and dancing. You may have to deal with a crowded bar as you make your way through to the main dining room, but when you get there, there will be no doubt that it was worth the effort. The room has an elegant, warm ambience, and, all year round, you can sit next to a duck pond. A large picture window overlooks a small pristine garden where ducks waddle by and swim. In the rear there is another area enclosed in glass that has statues and sculptures. The whole place is lovingly beautiful and conducive to sharing sweet nothings and perhaps even richer dishes of highly recommended Italian fare.

Upstairs is the Winter Dining Room, with a fireplace and a rock and tree garden enclosed in glass. There is also the Alex Room, with jazz and Broadway music every Wednesday through Saturday, where you can have a pre- or apres-dinner drink. Without question this is a flawless, total evening package for the both of you.

♦ *Romantic Warning:* For weekend nights it's advisable to make a reservation a week in advance for the main dining room.

ECCO
124 Chambers Street *at Church Street*
227-7074
Very Expensive

The neighborhood and this restaurant have absolutely nothing in common. Squeezed into a fairly shabby street scene is the magnificent room of Ecco, which, with its high ceiling and carved wood paneling, immediately takes you into another world once you pass the etched-glass doors. The food preparations are just as outstanding. (**Note:** Since this has, at times, been a see-and-be-seen spot, ask the waitperson for an out-of-the-way table. Or just direct your vision at each other and no one else in the room will matter anyway.)

FIORI
4 Park Avenue *at 34th Street*
686-0226
Moderate

Beautifully arched tiled ceiling, classic murals and terra-cotta tiled floors reminiscent of an Italian villa is the lofty setting for this premier New York restaurant. Perhaps it's a bit too noisy, even during off hours, but the popularity only attests to the quality, and, besides, the dining room is just gorgeous.

GRAZIELLA'S
2 Bank Street *at Greenwich Avenue*
924-9450
Moderate

Elegant Graziella's is a place which everyone seems to miss. It's a bit out of the way, but this small, angled room is serene and definitely unhurried. We spent a memorable evening there once, when we watched the room fill up and empty out again. I think it's one of the handsomest of the Italian spots, with perfect atmosphere and luscious food.

GROTTO AZZURRA

387 Broom *at Mulberry Street*
925-8775
Moderate

A very private time can be afforded here in an otherwise overly crowded section of the world. This is a real grotto, more than a few steps down into the terra firma. Around for many years, it must have served as a model for *"Hernando's Hideaway,"* which for you means that you should expect a sultry, candlelit meal.

LITTLE ITALY
Mulberry Street
Very Inexpensive to Very Expensive

I should warn you that there's not so much Italy left in Italy anymore. The old neighborhood has retreated to Mulberry Street and branched off a bit onto a few nearby arterials. What hasn't changed is that there are restaurants lining the streets which will exceed your wildest Italian fantasies. If you have the time, you can shop for the one to your liking by simply browsing the windows and menus that decorate each doorway. Here's a hint: Try one where no one is smoking and antipastos in the window make your hearts pound. Or just come for cappuccino and dessert in the caffes that are almost as numerous and authentically Italian as the restaurants.

MARCHI'S
251 East 31st Street *between 2nd & 3rd Avenues*
679-2494
Moderate

Strolling down this quiet street lined with small townhouses, a church and some brownstones, it's easy to miss Marchi's. When we first stumbled upon this restaurant, we felt like explorers making a discovery. We happened to glance down through lace-covered windows of what we thought was a lovely ground floor apartment and we noticed a table filled with well-dressed people dining grandly in a jovial atmosphere. The room was carpeted in a rich red plush with elaborate flower arrangements and oil paintings. It felt as if we were observing a private party in a Victorian dining room. This was New York, wasn't it? And what was this place, a private club? No awning or sign was evident. After a thorough search we found the entrance and we went inside. And a fabulous Italian feast followed, highlighted by impeccable service, a unique prix fixe, five-course meal (no ordering) which never varies, except in the smallest way. The handout they give you describing the meal strictly states that the Marchis have very definite ideas on how a fine meal should be served and it is for this reason you will not be served butter; *"butter leads to bread and too much bread and butter would only spoil your appetite."* We didn't miss the butter. The foods are sensual and fresh, from the antipasto to the lasagna to the appetizer, chicken, veal, fresh cheeses, dessert, Cristoli (fried sugar twists) and demitasse. This is a meal that will please the heart and soul.

Note: Reservations are suggested and jackets are required.

PAOLUCCI'S

149 Mulberry Street *near Grand Street*
226-9653
Moderate

This is one of the classic choices in Little Italy. Here, an informal atmosphere and good-humored (very Italian) service and fresh food can accent a memorable evening. One waiter told us: *"Sometimes they are in love, and sometimes they are not so much in love. The food and me, we try to help."*

PICCOLO MONDO

1269 1st Avenue *between 68th & 69th Streets*
249-3141
Expensive

Of all the Italian restaurants in New York (and there are almost as many as stars in the sky) this is indeed one of the great ones. I know an embarrassingly affectionate couple who can remember each of the anniversaries they spent in this old-world locale. It is truly a place where romantics flock when they want to be left to themselves and their pasta.

ROMA di NOTTE

137 East 55th Street *between Lexington & 3rd Avenues*
832-1128
Moderate to Expensive

My uncle told me about this restaurant, and at first I was skeptical. Not because I don't trust my uncle's taste; he happens to have very good taste. It's just that, well, uncles aren't supposed to be romantic, are they? Well, there goes that stereotype. Roma di Notte fits every criterion for romance I can think of; a nice-sized marble dance floor, beautiful music you can move to, intimate dining settings in hidden nooks throughout the restaurant, strolling singers with rich Italian voices and dancing, dancing, dancing. The food, if you ever get around to eating, is also excellent. It is one of the more reasonably priced places to dance and dine in the city. What more could you ask for?

TRATTORIA DELL'ARTE
200 West 57th Street *at 7th Avenue*
245-9800
Moderate

Trattoria Dell'Arte is a quiet, attractive, reasonably priced adventure in extremely desirable Italian cuisine. The lighting is soft, the interior is pastel, the tables are far enough apart to make dining an intimate experience and the decor, although it leans a bit to the neo-funky side, sets a mood which is affectionate and fun.

ZINNO
126 West 13th Street *at 6th Avenue*
924-5182
Expensive

Several small rooms that wind their way to the back of this restaurant, located on the ground floor of a brownstone, give many opportunities for dining in what could only be called intimate surroundings. The food is exceptional and the service impeccable. All you have to do is supply the words of love to set the right mood.

Japanese Kissing

There are two types of people who eat sushi and sashimi. The first type get the craving and feel that ravishing need to sample those sculpted mosaics of seaweed and fish. These fanatics sometimes condescend to dine with a companion just to be socially polite; whether you're there isn't so important — as long as the chef is. The other type of sushi personality — my type — is less possessed and enjoys the experience from a more graceful perspective. Do not expect a romantic evening if the person you are dining with is of the former mindset, but if your significant other agrees with you that a brief visit into a tradition that is as entertaining as it is mystical is worthwhile, then I would count on a special evening out. (**Romantic Warning:** Sushi and sashimi have been getting a lot of bad press lately. If you're concerned, our recommendation is to check with the New York Board of Health to see what their latest information is on the subject of eating raw fish, but don't forget that there are many other wonderful Japanese delicacies to order besides sushi and sashimi. I know for some of you that may be hard to believe, but it's true.)

NISHI NOHO
380 Lafayette Street *near East 4th Street*
677-8401
Moderate

As far from the standard, ubiquitous sushi restaurants as you can get, this dining room is as beautiful and as romance-engendering a place as you are likely to find anywhere in the city. If you have a (you'll forgive the pun) yen for good seafood in a dramatic setting of huge windows and a black and pink, intimate interior, then this is the place.

SERYNA
11 East 53rd Street *between 5th & Madison Avenues*
980-9393
Very, Very Expensive

This is as seriously Japanese as it is extremely expensive, but it is also refined, calming, authentic and delicious. Because of the superior Japanese dining to which this restaurant is dedicated, it will be an experience that your pocketbook and hearts will remember.

SHOGUN
951 2nd Avenue *between 50th & 51st Streets*
421-6844
Inexpensive to Moderate

Perhaps the best sushi bargain in the city and also a most lovely place. This small, unpretentious but classic Japanese restaurant has some of the freshest fish we've ever sampled and a tantalizing salmon teriyaki. The only problem is that once we go here we tend to keep returning and returning. Sushi-and-romance like this is a diet you can get used to easily.

Kosher Kissing

With all due respect to those of the Jewish faith who are Orthodox and eat strictly kosher, I know that in regard to the etiquette of modesty, you are not likely to find any demonstrative affectionate behavior taking place in public. But that is not to say that there isn't romance to be achieved through long discussions, long stares and long dinners out during the week or after Sabbath on Saturday night. The pleasure of eating, the pleasure of good company, the pleasure of loving conversation and a reliable *hashgachah** can make an evening out a *simcha** all on its own with just the two of you. And, if you are out on a first or second date, with the need for more *shiduchim**, and the atmosphere can help, why not?

*Definitions: Hashgachah — A Hebrew word that refers to the rabbinic authority who verifies that a restaurant or food product is indeed **glatt** (really) kosher. **Simcha** — A Hebrew word meaning joyous occasion. **Shiduchim** — A Hebrew word for matchmaking.

CHANTILLY'S
1105 Kings Highway, Brooklyn
(718) 627-7865
Inexpensive

Right in the middle of one of the least romantic areas of Brooklyn is this charming confectionery shop that serves coffee and kosher chocolates. The neighborhood may not be perfect — but for sweet words over very sweet delicacies, in a dainty atmosphere, you can't do much better than this, and it is a definite welcome change of pace from pizza and falafel.

CHEERS
120 West 41st Street *between Broadway & 6th Avenue*
840-8810
Expensive

Cheers has originated an interesting concept — it is a kosher Italian restaurant that serves meat without any dairy products (because to do otherwise would hardly be kosher). I prefer Italian dishes that have cheese (loads of Mozzarella and Parmesan) and no meat, but even so, I found the food at Cheers to be generously and, for the most part, creatively served, particularly the succulent, oversized veal chops. Plus, the atmosphere was pleasing and conducive to intimate conversations. The woman at the table next to us was served a special covered dish topped with a red rose which, when lifted, revealed an anniversary present.

Note: Sunday night tends to be family night and the atmosphere is not the same as what you will find during the week.

DIVA'S
306 East 81st Street *between 1st & 2nd Avenues*
650-1928
Expensive

This intimate, sometimes quiet, sometimes vibrant restaurant provides some of the best kosher dining in town. And if it wasn't for the board supervision framed on the outside you wouldn't know it was different from any other sophisticated, cozy, brick-walled dining room anyplace else in town. Open for dinner only, this is one of those true getaway locations when being in the center of things isn't what the two of you want to share for the evening.

MADRAS WOODLANDS
308 East 81st Street *between 1st & 2nd Avenues*
759-2440
Moderate

This is truly a beautiful, genteel *(not gentile)* dining room, with attentive waiters that are gracious and very polite. And the food! Well, it isn't what I would call traditional Jewish fare, but it is exotic, gourmet vegetarian cuisine, with unforgettable tastes and aromas. The tables are well spaced and the simple pink and gray decor is relaxing, and, in a traditional kind of way, romantic. Not your run-of-the-mill kosher fare, but for those with adventurous tastes, a unique dining experience for sure.

MY MOST FAVORITE DESSERT COMPANY
1165 Madison Avenue *at 86th Street*
517-5222
Inexpensive to Moderate

All right, I admit it, I'm a dessert lover and even if this place wasn't a classic cafe-styled restaurant with marble tabletops designed for two in a sweet unruffled atmosphere, I would still be a fan. Their desserts are outrageous examples of how sugar can be used to torment your taste buds to excess. Sometimes this is the only way to say good night, good morning, happy anniversary, happy birthday . . . it is always sweetly romantic. Oh, I almost forgot to mention that they make fresh, smooth quiches and excellent salads and pastas, but at the moment, it doesn't seem important.

PRIMAVERA
2086 Coney Island Avenue, Brooklyn
(718) 627-3904
Inexpensive

With all due respect to the management at Primavera, this Italian dining room isn't even vaguely romantic, nor does it look particularly Italian or Jewish or anything for that matter. So why am I writing about it? Because the food is amazingly fantastic and even more amazingly reasonable, which made us too full to feel anything even resembling romantic. Not every eating experience needs to foster intimate conversation; but perhaps, once you've eaten this well, you can discuss more personal matters on the way home.

Spanish/Mexican Kissing

For the most part, Spanish, and even more so, Mexican restaurants are casual, fun, carefree kinds of places for beer and margarita drinking, chip-dipping and loud conversation. That's all well and good; but for the purpose of this book, we really did our research to find those places that attend to the palate as well as your *muy grande* heart. We found a handful of romantic spots where, in between appetizers (tapas), you can enjoy a kiss to cool off the spices and peppers.

HARLEQUIN
569 Hudson Street *at West 11th Street*
255-4950
Moderate to Expensive

An exquisite location with a menu to match. The Spanish cuisine is well served here, and this one is one of my favorite romantic spots in the city. The decor is classic, but interesting with exotic touches, and the service is attentive and helpful.

MAXIMILIANO
208 East 52nd Street *at 3rd Avenue*
PL9-7373
Expensive

This is one of those places we kept passing on the way to work but never stopped at. It was right under our noses and we never knew what treats waited for us inside. The interior is elegant and the service formal but gracious and accommodating. Two unique appetizers were a generous meal by themselves, but the main course was divine. For a lunch-time getaway, even if it wasn't right around the corner from us, we would return again and again.

ROSA MEXICANA
1063 1st Avenue *at 58th Street*
753-7407
Moderate

When my friend showed me this place she said, just look and tell me if it's not wonderfully romantic. As usual, she was right. The back dining area was truly lovely. There is a stone fountain in the center overflowing with flowers. The room is softly lit. Rose-colored stucco walls create a pretty hue all about and huge floor vases are filled with even more flowers. This place is considered to be one of the prettiest and best Mexican restaurants in town. It also seems to be one of the best for couples who want to share the city's most superb guacamole and a sensational margarita with two straws.

> "BEAUTY IS HOW YOU FEEL INSIDE, AND IT REFLECTS IN YOUR EYES. IT IS NOT SOMETHING PHYSICAL OR UNDERSTOOD BY ANYONE ELSE BUT YOUR BELOVED."
>
> *Sophia Loren*

◆ Cabaret/Lounge Kissing ◆

R emember those late-night movies in black and white from the
'40s where hearts were lost, found, broken and mended all at a
quiet table in the corner of a jazz club or piano bar? There was always
dulcet music in the background which would swell just in time for
the lovers to engage in a tearful embrace with lyrics that fit the scene
perfectly — *"Play it again, Sam."* As cliched as it sounds, those
romantic moments are alive and well in New York City. Music lovers
here know there are almost too many nightlife possibilities to choose
from. Our list is only for those with tender thoughts. You won't find
hard rock or down-and-out funky blues listed here. Regardless of
taste, your modus operandi should be to check the *Village Voice* or
the *Times* to see who's playing where and make a reservation.

Note: Cabarets usually impose a cover or music charge, which can
range from about $10 – $25 per person, along with a two-drink
minimum. In some rooms dinner is available, but even a very expensive cabaret (if you don't dine) can prove more financially manageable
than a moderate restaurant for an evening out. (The price ratings
are based on a comparison of costs of all the places listed.)

THE BALLROOM
253 West 28th Street *between 7th & 8th Avenues*
244-3005
Expensive

There is no ballroom at The Ballroom, but there is incredible
music, excellent food and a suitable atmosphere for cuddling. This
is the well-known Spanish restaurant that is credited with starting
the tapas revolution. It is also credited with being one of the finest
cabarets in New York. Their headliners know how to render a love
song designed for those in love to understand.

CAFE LIDO — See Garvin's (Restaurants Continental)

THE CARLYLE CAFE — See The Carlyle Restaurant (Restaurants Continental)

DANNY'S SKYLIGHT ROOM at the GRAND SEA PALACE
346 West 46th Street *between 8th & 9th Avenues*
265-8130
Moderate

This is a more relaxed spot along restaurant row and it is unusual for a cabaret in that the food is very ethnic and very exceptional, served from the Thai kitchen of the Grand Sea Palace. They'll even apply the check to the cover charge. Come here for a quiet evening with some popular local chanteuse.

EIGHTY-EIGHTS
228 West 10th Street *at Bleecker Street*
924-0088
Inexpensive

This place is an intimate art deco room big enough for two handfuls of couples to cozy up to the piano and listen to some wonderful melodies and well-turned songs. (**Warning:** Make sure you go upstairs to the Cabaret Room, as downstairs is reserved for raucous sing-alongs.)

THE GRAND BAY HOTEL LOBBY LOUNGE
152 West 51st Street *between 7th Avenue & Broadway*
765-1900
Inexpensive

City life can provide many things for those in need of places to go, but the accessibility of cozy corners of the world that are private and nurturing can be difficult, if not almost impossible, to find, inside or out. What New York City doesn't lack even a little are those places for what has been coined the power lunch, dinner or drinks. All of that is fine and relatively exciting, particularly if Wall Street turns you on, but if you're in the mood for appreciative eye-gazing, then the choices get narrowed down. The Grand Bay Hotel, in spite of its *power* location, lacks a grandiose lobby area and, therefore, has just the right prerequisites for an intimate repose. This quiet, calm corner of the city, painted in pale tones of tan and heather, with velvety sofas and snuggly chairs, is an inviting spot that most times of day will provide a tender backdrop in which to rendezvous before or after anything you're about to do.

GREENE STREET CAFE
101 Greene Street *at Spring Street*
925-2415
Expensive

This is a cabaret that calls itself a cafe, which is really stretching things. No one would mistake it for anything other than a high-brow, formal restaurant in the truest sense of the words. It is perhaps too slick to be romantic, but the extremely tall ceiling, large wicker chairs, spot-lit trees, a really excellent (very pricey) menu and (what makes it all worthwhile) the entertaining contemporary jazz sounds make this place totally irresistible. Greene's has a cabaret at 105 Greene Street on the top floor, Friday and Saturday nights only.

THE GRILL ROOM at the DORAL HOTEL
70 Park Avenue *at 11th Avenue*
687-7050
Expensive

The newest room in town is The Grill Room. The wood paneling and good dinner here provide all you need for a quiet, cozy evening at the top of Murray Hill. The romance potential here is higher than at most places, so let's hope this one sticks around.

THE HUNT BAR at the HELMSLEY PALACE HOTEL
455 Madison Avenue *at 50th Street*
888-7000
Inexpensive

Believe me, it is not my desire to give Leona Helmsley any more press than she already buys for herself, but the truth of it is that the Hunt Bar is one of the most intimate, handsome bars in New York and it happens to be located at the lavish Helmsley Palace Hotel. What a genuinely exquisite setting to rendezvous in before, during or after a busy day. There are only a handful of seats in this small, intimate hideaway, either on damask-covered stools at the rich wood bar or on the satin-striped sofas within warm view of the massive carved fireplace. The interior design of the Hunt Bar seems more appropriately placed in *Architectural Digest* than showcased in a tucked-away corner of this hotel, but here it is nonetheless. The paneled walls and ceiling are truly superb examples of brilliant craftsmanship and detailing. The entire effect is one of being entwined in another era.

J's
2581 Broadway *at 97th Street*
758-2272
Inexpensive to Moderate

An out-of-the-way, extremely cozy, reasonably priced cabaret (no cover, $10 minimum), serving excellent Continental cuisine and always serving up excellent entertainment — one of the places to run away to frequently to have yourselves lulled gently into a loving New York frame of mind.

L'OMNIBUS CAFE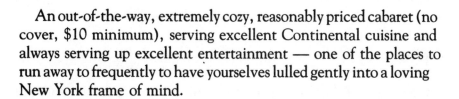
680 Madison Avenue *at 61st Street*
751-5111
Expensive to Very Expensive (for dinner only)

L'Omnibus presents the height of Parisian elegance, with prices to match, but few venues in New York can claim as seductive a setting. The room is provocatively lit by candles in flowered sconces, and murals depicting femmes fatales in alluring haute couture set the mood. Attention is centered on the two or three shows nightly, offering cafe-society piano renditions of classic songs (Cole Porter, *"La Vie en Rose,"* etc.) performed by first-rate entertainers. Definitely serious romancing here.

Supper is available, but drinks or coffee and dessert seem more appropriate and will help keep the tab within reason. If you're there for the latter, try some of the outstanding French patisserie displayed on a dessert cart. Service is unusually cordial for a place so chi-chi, and they'll even sing happy anniversary if you request it. Reservations are advisable. Save this one for a very special occasion.

Note: Cover charge is $15 per person, and there's no minimum.

◆ *Romantic Option:* Upstairs at the sensual, dazzling **Maxim's** restaurant you'll find another charming place to rendezvous, with dining and dancing to a five-piece orchestra — that's arm-in-arm, close, hip guiding, rhythmic dancing, the way it should be done.

MICHAEL'S PUB
211 East 55th Street *between 2nd & 3rd Avenues*
758-2272
Expensive

Good food and great singers make this a sure bet for a wonderful night out. If you're looking for something truly memorable on the East Side, you've come to the right spot. (Yes, this is where Woody Allen plays clarinet on Monday nights, not necessarily romantic, but interesting.)

OAK ROOM at the ALGONQUIN HOTEL
59 West 44th Street *between 5th & 6th Avenues*
840-6800
Expensive

There was almost no place in New York I wanted more to write about than the Algonquin because two dear friends of mine, Brian Lasser and Karen Mason, had their opening there in March when I scheduled my romantic visit. I've known these talented people for almost 20 years and their performances tend to bring heaven down to earth for the evening, which made me concerned about just how objective I could be. In light of these circumstances, to be safe, I went again when they weren't performing just to be sure I wouldn't be biased one way or the other.

Aesthetically and amorously the best of the best is the Oak Room. Those who know the New York cabaret scene know that this is the place. The dark wood paneling and gracious, intimate atmosphere help to create lasting memories. You can get very cozy sitting side-by-side on the long banquette, lining the sides of the room. (By the way, my friends opened to rave reviews, including mine.)

ONE FIFTH AVENUE BAR — See Marylou's (Restaurants American)

PIER 17 at the SOUTH STREET SEAPORT — See Miscellaneous Kissing

RAINBOW ROOM — See Restaurants Continental

ROMA di NOTTE — See Restaurants Italian

TOP of the TOWERS
3 Mitchell Place *at 49th Street & 1st Avenue*
(in the Beekman Tower Hotel)
355-7300
Inexpensive

New York is probably the most romantic when you're high above it gazing down at those things that are usually bothersome when you're there in the thick of it. Bumper-to-bumper honking cars, neon lights emanating from building after monolithic building and the endless promenade of people soften and take on an ethereal quality at heights reserved for birds and those with apartment views. In terms of kissing places with this attraction, there are many scattered in the skyscrapers that make up this city's lofty, dense personality, but none is as secluded and quintessentially romantic as the cocktail lounge at the top of the Beekman Tower Hotel.

The Top of the Towers has a 360-degree view of Midtown's East Side and this is without question wondrous and spectacular. And the interior, with or without the view, would be cozy enough for even the most skeptical New Yorker to find enchanting. A few well-spaced tables, designed mostly for two, circle around a small aisle, nestled against the perimeter of the stone-encased tower. Each table has its own ringside view with only a small candle for light (the rest of the illumination dances through the windows from the city beyond). The open-air balcony is available in balmy weather for outside seating and is definitely a viable option when the nighttime air feels like the sun is still shining (although those suffering from vertigo might want to reconsider). Gentle, unobtrusive piano music begins after 9 p.m.

Note: There is no cover charge, but the drinks are fairly high, over $6 each. Espressos are priced at $4.00. It is also strongly advised to call before going lest a private party to which you haven't been invited has closed the tower for the evening.

WINDOWS on the WORLD HORS D'OEUVRERIE 💋💋💋
One World Trade Center
938-1111
Moderate to Expensive

Although this is the perfect place to go to spontaneously, you must choose the night carefully. If it's rainy, cloudy, foggy or overcast, get thee to a dark nightclub and not to this breathtaking cocktail lounge perched 107 floors above the sparkly city. On the other hand, if the evening is about to descend on a clear day, there may be no more enchanting, breathtaking place to witness the event than the Hors D'oeuvrerie (as captivating as it is difficult to spell).

The room is perfectly lit. The sometimes noisy bar is tucked away behind swinging saloon doors. There are abundant tables for two beside the omnipresent windows, and the sounds of a melodic keyboard in the background. All that alone would be enough to enhance a loving tryst, but as you may already know, the appeal of the Hors D'oeuvrerie doesn't stop there. Looking west from that height, red sunsets really do exist as the buildings change from their daytime business dress to their elegant evening wear. Of all the view experiences this city has to bestow, this one soars above the rest in dimension as well as quality.

Note: Ignore the popularity of the name and come here most anytime except weekends, when everyone else comes here, and sit at heights normally reserved for angels. Breakfast is available every day, but the atmosphere tends to be more business oriented. Sunday brunch is an extravagant, excellent choice. But the view, oh that view, it can create any atmosphere you need during your visit and render time an affair of hearts and eyes.

> "IN THEIR CHOICE OF LOVERS, BOTH THE MALE AND
> FEMALE REVEAL THEIR ESSENTIAL NATURE.
> THE TYPE OF HUMAN BEING WHICH WE PREFER
> REVEALS THE CONTOURS OF OUR HEART."
>
> *Jose Ortega y Gasset*

◆ Outdoor Kissing ◆

BARGEMUSIC — See River Cafe (Restaurants American)

BRONX BOTANICAL GARDENS
(212) 220-8777

Located in the Bronx Park, which they share with the Zoo, the Gardens are neighbors with Fordham University, where Mosholu and Pelham Parkways and Fordham Road come together. Metro North Station from Manhattan runs a special which includes admission to the Conservatory.

The Gardens make a brilliant backdrop for romance when they blaze with their unending variety of flowers, but thanks to the steamy Conservatory, Mother Nature and Sonny Boy Cupid, they can be visited all year round. From the first daffodils of April, through the red, red roses of late September, the warmer months are the best time to take your dreams to this earthly paradise. Whether your flower-madness compels you and your beloved to sniff away at the tens of thousands of blooms, or your wanderlust leads you over the green knolls and meadows, or your gentler sentiments incline you to find a shady tree, the Gardens have something for both of you.

You might want to know that it's not all carefully cultivated dahlias and dogwood here: nature primeval is also to be found. The only virgin forest left in New York City stands here by the gorge which the rapid Bronx River has cut through the rocks over a course of centuries. Right near the dramatic falls of the river, you can dine at the Old Mill and feel that you're in a quaint New England town miles away from city life.

◆ *Romantic Options:* You can easily stroll across Fordham Road to visit either the University (don't miss the Chapel, whose bells inspired Edgar Allen Poe to write *"Annabelle Lee"* — their cottage stands nearby) or the zoo, officially the **New York Zoological**

Gardens, (212) 367-1010 — one of the largest zoos in the world and probably one of the best. You shouldn't underestimate the charms of the animal kingdom. The zoo's two nature rides, one called Skyfari, can provide some quiet moments complete with *"Out of Africa"* scenery and soundtrack. You won't be the only ones here, particularly when summer vacation is in effect. But once you've started your trek around this paradise, all you'll see are the animals and each other. When you've finished, if you have a car, you must drive back over Fordham Road and turn left to the Arthur Avenue Historic District to dine at some of the best Italian restaurants in the city.

BRONX RIVER PARKWAY PATH

The path extends from Bronxville north to the Kensico Dam in Valhalla, Westchester. Take FDR Drive in Manhattan north, cross East River on Willis Avenue Bridge to Major Deegan Highway (Route 87), north to Cross County Parkway, east to Bronx River Parkway, north to Bronxville or other towns. One half-hour mid-Manhattan to Bronxville.

What a wonderful piece of wilderness remains in Westchester. Conservationists and romanticists alike are proud and delighted at the foresight of the creators of this ten-mile park. Those in need of refuge from the city will find it to be a desirable place to enjoy peace and togetherness.

A wide stretch on each side of the Bronx River Parkway has been maintained in its original pristine, sylvan state, safeguarded for the pleasures of those who relish nature and woods undisturbed by civilization. In recent years, a paved path winding through this park has been handsomely constructed between Bronxville and Valhalla. It is ideal for arm-in-arm touring or bicycling about the countryside together. The terrain is varied along the path, except for the bubbling Bronx River, which will accompany you most of the way. Many parts are secluded, and the two of you could well imagine yourselves to be in a remote section of the Adirondacks. In direct contrast, other sections are wide open including a spacious grassy area in Bronxville with an aqua-blue pond filled with seasonal birds and occasional swans. There are a few benches along the way, where you can sit and talk, or just rest, or whatever suits your purpose.

Note: The Kensico Dam area at the northern end of the path has some dramatic points of interest. The dam and surrounding grounds were artistically designed, although their maintenance has been less than perfect. A brick road winds through the woods up to the top of the dam, which provides an all-encompassing view of Westchester to the south and the beautiful Kensico Reservoir to the north. Cars as well as hikers can easily traverse the top of the dam. Also, the Parkway is closed to autos every Sunday in May through October from 10 a.m. to 2 p.m.

♦ *Romantic Warning:* The Parkway goes through several suburban towns, the paved path continues all the way except through Scarsdale, which can be walked through on side roads. At the White Plains Station, the path becomes a quiet road for about one-quarter mile. The path also stops at the North White Plains station, where one must walk through a parking lot to reach the resumption of the path.

♦ *Romantic Option:* If you are hungry in or near White Plains, you can find a cozy lunch or dinner at **Gregory's Restaurant, 324 Central Avenue, White Plains (914) 428-2455** (Moderate to Expensive). Just north of White Plains Station, you will see a large building, the Westchester County Center, and its parking lot. Gregory's is one-third mile south from there on Route 100 (Central Avenue). The one-third mile walk is not in the least bit romantic, but the restaurant is. The interior of the renovated old house with weathered wood walls and beamed ceilings dramatize the nautical setting. With soft lights, a quiet atmosphere and flowers on each table, it is a comfortable place to enjoy the pleasures of the food and time with your companion. (The menu encompasses Continental and Italian specialties.)

BROOKLYN BOTANIC GARDEN
1000 Washington Avenue
(718) 622-4433

From Manhattan, take the Manhattan Bridge, go straight on Flatbush Avenue to Grand Army Plaza, then follow Eastern Parkway to a right on Washington Avenue.

These gardens are a 50-acre oasis of pastoral splendor and tranquility in the midst of the bustling borough of Brooklyn. Bring a special someone and dreams to share as you discover the winding and secluded paths, throw pennies into sparkling fountains, stretch out on the grass while gazing upward at a full blue sky, or listen to the rush of a rocky stream. The Garden itself is comprised of many smaller gardens within a forest, and so you are sure to find a special, always to be remembered spot, just for the two of you.

On a grand scale, the Cranford Rose Garden, with formal walkways leading to a latticed white portico at one end, is, in the months of June and September, an elegantly wondrous tribute to romance's own true flower. In April and May the Cherry Esplanade, with its rows of wildly pink blossoms, cheerfully heralds the spring. Smaller, more intimate spaces include the Shakespeare Garden, an English country-cottage setting for the collection of flowers mentioned in Will's plays and sonnets, and the Fragrance Garden, beds of flowers that can be savored by the senses of smell and vision. And there's so much more: the Rock Garden, the Iris Garden and Daffodil Hill, all surrounded by dogwoods, rhododendrons, ash trees and honeysuckle, willow and witch hazel, snowdrops and conifers, stately oaks and beeches. There is also the Steinhardt Conservatory, a miracle of urban architecture and horticultural design. The glass pavilions allow you to pass through a steamy tropical forest, a Mediterranean hillside and a scorching desert. Around the world in an afternoon, smack dab in the middle of Brooklyn.

Perhaps the most beautiful location is the Japanese Hill and Pond Garden. When you pass through the bamboo gates, you enter a world of timeless harmony and craftsmanship. Once inside, winding, narrow pathways take you around the reflecting lake, toward vantage points high and low, past Japanese lanterns, over small stone bridges and up a grassy, secluded hill to a Buddhist shrine. Here everything is appropriately symbolic: tall pines suggest longevity and the rock formations signify strength; even the shape of the lake represents the Japanese symbol for heart and mind.

◆ *Romantic Suggestion:* The Garden's Patio Restaurant (Inexpensive), overlooking the Fragrance Garden, offers refreshment in spring and summer.

Note: The Brooklyn Botanic Garden is very popular at cherry-blossom time and on high-summer weekends. However, the enforcement of strict noise- and recreational restrictions, as well as the presence of many out-of-the-way spaces and less-traveled by-ways, mean that romantic interludes are rarely, if ever, hard to come by.

THE BROOKLYN BRIDGE

The bridge spans the East River joining Manhattan and Brooklyn. Leave the car and take the subway. To reach the Manhattan side of the bridge take the 4,5 or 6 to the Brooklyn Bridge, or the 1,2 or 3.

This isn't the longest bridge in the city, but it's certainly the most beautiful. Walking over the venerable Brooklyn Bridge is an exhilarating experience. Here you can feel the impact of the city in the air, neither encumbered nor fenced in by buildings. Here you can walk above it all and take the astonishingly spectacular view in at the same time.

Probably the most convenient and provocative way to enjoy your own trek across the span is to start at City Hall Park. The park is pleasant anytime, but in the warm months, its gardens are in full bloom and the serene, white fountain cools the area with a light refreshing spray. From here, you can't miss the bridge towering above you. Cross Park Row and find the kiosk labeled *"Bridge Footpath."*

Then go down the steps. Once on the footpath, you'll have a clear view up to the middle point of the Bridge's bow shape. As you're lifted high above the city streets, be sure to look down at the canyons of Wall Street and the forest masts on the tall ships of South Street Seaport. From the middle of the Bridge, look upward toward the Manhattan skyline, and don't forget to remind each other to breathe. There are benches along the way where you can snuggle in the breeze and, depending on the time of day, you'll have the pathway all to yourselves. Early in the morning or toward twilight, the glistening waters of the harbor and the proud silhouette of the Statue of Liberty are unforgettable.

◆ *Romantic Warning:* There's a reason it took 250 years for New Yorkers to build a bridge over the river: *It's a long way!* The walk takes about 30 to 45 minutes.

BROOKLYN HEIGHTS — See River Cafe (Restaurants American)

CARL SCHURZ PARK

East End Avenue from 84th to 89th Street

Tucked away next to the East River on the very edge of upper Manhattan, this quiet little park has been a haven for lovers to get away to for as long as I can remember. Walk up the semicircular stairway at 86th Street to the promenade. To the north, you'll see the twinkling strands of lights which mark the Triboro Bridge, and, far away to the south, those of the Queensboro Bridge. In the trees behind you, you'll hear flocks of birds providing a musical background to your walk. The most special moments come at dusk in winter, when you can walk hand in hand with a special other along the wide, curving promenade overlooking the water and witness the change of day across the sky.

In spring, the flower beds are full of tulips and daffodils and the entry to this park is lined with cherry trees abloom in pink. In fall, the autumn air is crisp and the leaves are as colorful as any you'll see this far south of New England. In summer, the benches are a great place for a picnic as you watch the movement of ships along the river. At the south end of the park there is a playing field and playground; both are sometimes used for summer evening concerts.

◆ *Romantic Warning:* On warm, sunny days, especially in spring and summer, everybody in the neighborhood comes out to get a tan or play. Though Carl Schurz is still a fun place under these circumstances, quiet is no longer the right word.

CENTRAL PARK

Between 59th and 110th Streets and 5th Avenue and Central Park West

For those who know how to safely handle this vast acreage of city park it can be as if Central Park and romance were, themselves, a loving couple. The aroma of chestnuts, the sight of couples huddled warmly in horse-drawn carriages or strolling hand-in-hand by the sailboat pond amid the blossoming cherry trees, or listening to the carousel's piping calliope or just sitting admiring the theatrical celebration that overflows from almost every corner such things prove to be joys any time of day or year. *There is so much to see;* lakes and broad lawns, quaint wrought-iron street lamps alongside curving walks, lofty hardwood trees, granite outcroppings and the electric atmosphere of cosmopolitan Manhattan nearby. When you experience the park's endless, varied sensations — watching street performers at **Bethesda Terrace** (mid-park at 72nd) or hearing the Philharmonic on the **Great Lawn** (mid-park at 81st) or taking in sunshine wherever feels the most comfortable — you will most assuredly have your prelude to romance.

What could be more enlivening to your senses on a frosty day than to glide together at the **Wollman Ice Rink** and then share a steaming hot chocolate while watching the colorful parade of the graceful and the clumsy pass by. Or on a fragrantly warm and sunny day, you could rent a boat at **Loeb Boathouse**. Paddle out onto the lake and then drift along under the formidable stone and wooden bridges, or along the shore by the lanquid willows catching a glimpse of the distant buildings through the green drooping leaves. There are many modes of transportation in Central Park besides boats, skates or hansom cabs; you can also try a bicycle-built-for-two, available for rent at Loeb Boathouse. A cut-through for cyclists exists between East and West Drives, with a lawn sloping down toward a lovely wooded glen.

The Conservatory Garden is another special, quiet place in the park just off 5th Avenue at 105th Street. It is the only formal garden here, and actually is three separately designed plantings — one has the Untermeyer Fountain as its centerpiece, another is dotted with statues of storybook characters, and the third is flanked by two stately, trellised archways covered in aromatic wisteria vines. This section of Central Park is truly one of the magical spots of the city.

Note: The numerous attractions and activities offered in Central Park are far more than can be listed here. Call the **Visitor Center at 397-3156** to find out the day's happenings.

CITY ISLAND, Bronx

Take the Triboro Bridge toward the Bronx. Follow Bruckner Expressway (Route 278) north. Exit at 8B: Orchard Beach/City Island. Follow the road, bearing right at the traffic light. Well-marked signs point the way to City Island. About 30-45 minutes from Manhattan.

From October through April, our favorite mini-holiday is a sunny afternoon on City Island — an unpretentious New England whaling village off the coast of the Bronx. Here you can take your time looking at sailboats, water and soothing scenery. City Island is tiny, about a mile long and very narrow. You can easily walk or bike the length of City Island Avenue, from the bridge to the mainland, all the way to Long Island Sound. If you love boats, this is paradise. Old and new marine gear abounds and the area is lined with boat yards and shops. The village even has a sailmaker.

Quiet residential streets run east and west off City Island Avenue. With the bridge behind you, turn right on any byway. Every street ends at a private **(warning:** *private means private***)** beach facing the Manhattan skyline, across Eastchester Bay. Small-town America is so apparent you expect Mickey Rooney and Judy Garland to dash out of a one-family home.

◆ *Romantic Suggestion:* Restaurants line City Island Avenue. For lunch, try **Anna's Harbor Restaurant, 565 City Island Avenue, (212) 885-1373** (Moderate), with its huge, glass-enclosed dining area jutting into the bay. Filled with plants, it has the feel of a greenhouse on a harbor. Eat lunch and watch the boats or come for an early dinner and see the sunset.

◆ *Romantic Warning:* If you head for City Island in summer, expect traffic, crowds and limited parking spaces. Off season is definitely the more romantic time to visit here. Also, don't bother going to City Island unless you plan to eat a meal — a seafood meal that is.

CLOISTERS/FORT TRYON PARK
(212) 923-3700

At 192nd between Riverside Drive & Fort Washington Avenue

The most romantic thing about the Cloisters is not the Cloisters, which officially refers to the Cloisters Museum, the medieval branch of the Metropolitan Museum of Art. (The museum has been assembled stone by stone from European monasteries and closely resembles the real thing. It is indeed beautiful and interesting but a little too austere and religious to be defined as a smooching location.) Rather, the romance is to be found in Fort Tryon Park, the giant sprawling home to the museum. With its hours of meandering river and wood trails, chirping birds (yes, there are birds that chirp in Manhattan), panoramic vistas, towering trees, herb gardens and, in the springtime, flowers, flowers, flowers, the park is a New York-style fairy tale.

Upon entering the park at the very end of Fort Washington Avenue, you'll be immediately confronted with a difficult choice: which beckoning path to take. My husband's favorite option is to do it all. First, linger around the short garden path which will be directly in front of you. Something about that path has always struck me as surreal. It is difficult to tell where the colors of the leaves and flowers end and the Hudson River Palisades backdrop begins. Next, take the river route by following the stone wall around toward the left. In a few minutes, you will see the Cloisters themselves in the distance. When you get to the museum, stop in and see the famous Unicorn Tapestries and rest in the central open-air garden courts, the lower court featuring herbs and the upper a plethora of flowers. Then, take the woodsy route back past the Unicorn Cafe, which on a balmy day is kind of a sweet place to sojourn over a cup of coffee. If you take the circular route, you will eventually find yourself reluctantly back at the entrance. Depending on the season, you'll find several spots to satisfy your kissing inclinations.

◆ *Romantic Option:* If you keep walking north past the Cloisters, you will come to **Inwood Park**, and there are trails that will take you down to the river.

◆ *Romantic Warning:* This is a city park. If you look too closely you will see signs of wildlife: graffiti, litter and minor vandalism. And, although after many years of exploring this park I've never observed any problems, a romantic park warning is part and parcel of New York life. But don't let that stop you. You can always keep to areas where people are concentrated.

COLUMBIA UNIVERSITY

Main Gate, 116th Street & Broadway

Those who think that wandering above 100th Street is only for people who can't count or don't know any better are missing out on something special and should consider breaking tradition to see what lies a little further beyond. For the young, the young at heart and those who wholeheartedly cherished their college years, long forgotten memories of campus life are certain to return as you ramble through the ivory towers of Columbia University. Replete with history and echoes of the classical past, this hallowed institution offers appealing architecture, wide-open grounds to picnic on, great student-watching and a few hidden corners in which to indulge a kiss or two. Depending on the season, there's no telling what activities you'll stumble across on campus: perhaps a concert of ethnic music, a crafts fair or, believe it or not, a political demonstration, not like the ones we used to have, but a rally is a rally. There are always Frisbee games of various skill levels going on, the foolish frolicking of students (yes, students still frolic, didn't you?) and sun lovers stretched out soaking up the warmth whenever the skies are clear. Why not join them? You're only young for the rest of your lives.

♦ *Romantic Option:* **Riverside Church Bell Tower and Observatory, Riverside Drive** *between 120th and 122nd Streets*, is the ideal place to go with someone who is passionate about celestial views and heavenly music. From the 20th floor, you'll climb 147 steps (trust me, it's worth it) through a 74-bell carillon where hypnotically beautiful concerts are performed every Sunday. An observation deck provides a 360-degree panorama where you can pause for an elevated kiss, but don't neglect the spectacular views in all directions.

FOREST HILLS GARDENS, Queens

Take Interborough Parkway heading east and take the Forest Hills exit heading north into Forest Hills.

Although I'm not the type who usually recommends ogling homes belonging to people who are more likely to speak of the number of wings on their residences than the number of rooms, once you swallow your envy, a brisk or lazy walk through the estates of this neighborhood can be an enticing pleasure. After cruising through the web of twisting roads that lace the astonishing architecture, together you can easily stroll from the gardens into the nearby park, where the overlook is a favorite place to kiss. After all that walking, ice cream, cappuccino or a bite to eat is certain to appeal, and I enthusiastically recommend a detour to the **Metro Soda Fountain, 116-02 Metropolitan Avenue (718) 846-8787** (Inexpensive). The Fountain has been fastidiously restored to its original detail, complete with etched glass, art deco molding and pressed tin ceilings. The lighting is warm and rosy, the music is vintage 1940s. Tasty sandwiches and salads are served here, but the soda fountain's most distinguishing feature is its ice cream menu. My husband likes the copious peanut butter sundaes, and I go for the traditional banana split, which is, unfortunately, equally copious and sinful.

FRANCIS LEWIS PARK, Queens

Take the Whitestone Expressway (678) to the last exit before the toll. After the exit, turn right on 3rd Avenue, which will dead end at the park.

Not what anyone would call a comely park, but for those who love searching out classic views of Manhattan, this one should not be missed. It is rarely crowded and is, for a city spot, beautiful. The Whitestone looms overhead, and the sound of the cars racing by resembles the sound of ocean surf. The lawn sweeps down to water's edge where a few park benches are scattered about here and there in discreet distance from each other. And then there's the view of the city, a vibrant living sculpture that is impossible to do justice to in describing. But after you've seen it, it will be something you'll never forget.

JAMAICA BAY WILDLIFE REFUGE
Cross Bay Boulevard, Queens
(718) 338-3799

From Manhattan, follow the Belt Parkway to Exit 17. Cross Bay Boulevard and head south toward Rockaway across the North Channel Bridge. The Refuge is one mile past the bridge on the right.

This is one of the great hidden gems of New York City: an island of greenery in a sea of concrete. Although it is hard to be entirely alone here, somehow we never find the company of egrets, ospreys, owls, woodpeckers, herons and swans (to name a few) terribly intrusive. Even the Audubon loyalists who flock here don't disturb our privacy because there are plenty of secret escapes just off the main trail. Following the two-mile West Pond Trail down toward the water, where it winds between the bay and a manmade freshwater pond, you can watch the horizon shift continually. Around one bend the Verrazano Bridge comes into view, and around another, the Twin Towers and the Empire State Building suddenly loom large. Near the end of the loop a sign points back to the visitor center. If you turn off the main trail at that point, you'll find a spider web of small paths that meander through birch groves and holly bushes, where few visitors venture and the privacy is yours alone.

The mood of the Refuge changes with the season, but it retains a romantic spell all year round. Spring and fall are a bird watcher's delight, when feathered friends are migrating between breeding grounds high in the Canadian Arctic and winter hideaways in Central and South America. When the bitter (or mild) winter seems to go on endlessly, urban-weary New Yorkers can find solace in nature's stark beauty. And in summertime, when *hot* feels like an understatement, there is comfort here in the cooling sea breezes that blow gently across the countryside.

♦ *Romantic Option:* If an Irish coffee or a spirit-warming cognac sounds like it would hit the spot after your day at the Refuge, you can nicely meet that need plus enjoy a full, tempting seafood dinner

at **Pier 92 Restaurant, 377 Beach 92nd Street, Rockaway Beach,
(718) 945-2200** (Moderate to Expensive). Head south down Cross
Bay Boulevard and onto Rockaway Peninsula in search of this place.
No signs mark the restaurant, but insiders look for the McDonald's
next door as a landmark. The Pier sports a crackling fire during the
winter, outdoor tables in the summer and, at all times, spectacular
views across Jamaica Bay to Kennedy Airport.

LONG ISLAND CITY WATERFRONT, Queens

*Driving from Manhattan, take the upper roadway of the Queensboro Bridge
to the 21st Street exit. Turn left on 21st and right on 44th Drive to the
end. From Queens and points east, follow any major Queens artery
westward, avoiding entrances to bridges and tunnels, to Vernon Boulevard,
which parallels the shoreline.*

Those definitive, intensely romantic views of the Mid-Manhattan
skyline and the Queensboro Bridge common to a score of movies
you've surely seen dozens of times are captured in person here. In
the background, the wondrous shapes of steel, the world center of
commerce and culture, expressed in soaring architecture; in the
foreground, the East River and, by day, the Gothic ruins of Roosevelt
Island. After dark, the building dimensions and textures yield to a
mesmerizing light show — the formal dress of the city: the Chrysler
in art deco elegance, the Empire State with its tricolor personality,
Citicorp's signature statement, the bridge wearing a sparkling
diamond necklace. A place to take it all in and yet be very much alone.

Two favorite outdoor locations provide marvelous vantage points
with considerable privacy. The cement pier at the foot of 44 Drive
juts over the water for the most spectacular view. About a half-mile
to the north, Queens Bridge Park is a more pastoral setting with
overwhelming closeups of the bridge. Plus, there are two stunning
restaurants (see Romantic Suggestions below) that provide the same
captivating view.

♦ *Romantic Suggestion:* **The Water's Edge, East River Yacht Club, East River and 44 Drive, Long Island City, Queens, (718) 482-0033** (Expensive), adjacent to the pier, is lavishly appointed and offers an expensive, mostly seafood, Continental menu. Live piano music, experienced, professional service, outdoor garden seating when weather permits and the view of Manhattan as the backyard setting can help assist anyone's romantic tastes. For a more moderate choice, **Doubbles Restaurant, 44th Avenue and Vernon Boulevard, (718) 937-3001** (Moderate), a long block north of the pier, is part of the East River Tennis Club complex. It is mostly business-oriented during the day. My favorite time to go is during long steamy summer evenings. When the sun bathes the city in a warm embrace, dinner is served outdoors and features broiled and barbecued favorites. The Club becomes a friendly, easygoing Long Island retreat, grass-carpeted down to the river with the urban mecca glistening across the water.

POCKET PARKS

I introduced this book with a romantic quote that speaks directly to the major problem New Yorkers face when it comes to romance (one of the major problems for anyone who lives in a big city): "*As usual with most lovers in the city — they were troubled by the lack of that essential need of love — a meeting place.*" Hopefully that is what you're finding in these pages, but this particular section speaks to that dilemma most eloquently. The pocket parks we've included contain prodigious amounts of greenery, privacy, views, singing birds and walking room inside a near-country-like space. Most important, they provide a meeting place where the two of you can get to know one another a little better than you did before. (The following entries are all pocket parks ending with Washington Market Square.)

Battery Park City
Along the Hudson on Rector Street

The green space at this park is both an esplanade and a park. The whole complex has been generously and thoughtfully landscaped. A square is set in the midst of the handsome post-modern apartment buildings, and the foliage continues down along the water. The view right across the river (New Jersey rustbelt) is, to put it kindly, nothing special, but the long view down to the harbor is impressive indeed. In the winter months you will likely see a string of sleek, white, grandiose vessels taking cruisers to the Caribbean or South America. In the warmer months, this is a favorite haunt of swift-going sailboats. The park, though, is at its best at twilight when the city behind you is glistening, and the water takes on a coppery glow. If you stay until the light dies down, you'll find some solitude in which to pass the beginnings of a balmy summer evening. (Open all year.)

Damrosch Park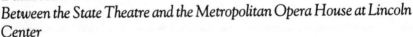
Between the State Theatre and the Metropolitan Opera House at Lincoln Center

This park is a surprisingly colorful corner of Manhattan that somehow escapes all the tourist traffic. You could certainly create a picnic outing from any of the delis on Broadway and camp here for the afternoon. It's very cozy under the trees, and if you think *"Music be the food of Love,"* then stay for one of the free summer concerts. This one is worth a special visit. Even the corresponding space formed by Fisher Hall, the Opera House and the Juilliard School is, with its pool and trees, one of the most elegant squares in New York.

Greenacre Park
221 East 51st Street *between 1st and 2nd Avenues*

What people think of when they hear the term *"vest-pocket parks"* is captured at this particular city oasis. Literally nestled between thick granite walls, this qualifies nicely as a refuge from the assaults of urban life. The small tables and chairs (as opposed to the common fixed benches) and the crystal-clear waterfall rushing over large stones and rocks give this spot a true European flair. You can sidle your chair right up to your companion's, and commence with the matters of the heart. There is even a small refreshment stand inside the gate. (**Note:** Closed for two months in the winter.)

Paley Plaza
3 East 53rd Street *between 5th and Madison Avenues*

Perhaps too small to even be considered a pocket park, this is a small change of scenery where you least expect it. If you're in the area it is a reprieve from the world at large, breathing space where the sounds of a waterfall replace the traffic noise and the cooling spray can revitalize any hot summer interlude.

Sutton Place Park
At East 57th Street and Sutton Place

If the evening is pleasant and there's romance in the air, stroll over to Sutton Place Park at the eastern end of 57th Street. After dark, the river is aglow with reflections of light from the opposite shore, and the stately Queensboro Bridge is handsomely outlined with its own necklace of illumination. Most couples linger by the railing awhile, watching the tugs and tankers silently ply the waters. The park offers an ample number of benches for snuggling, a fair amount of privacy, and is in one of the city's safest neighborhoods. What's more, you can enjoy this hideaway until its 1 a.m. closing time.

♦ *Romantic Warning:* This is strictly an after-dark venue for the amorous. During the day, the park is overrun by toddlers and their nannies doing everything but the things you would call romantic.

St. Paul's Chapel
Broadway at Vessey

If you think of churchyards as quaint, you may find this one to be a very peaceful oasis in the city. The charm of the 18th-century church and the old shade trees shelter you from the surrounding streets. Many romances of Old New York can be traced by reading the stones and the information plaques provided. (Open all year during church hours.)

Washington Market Square
Greenwich Street at Reade

This is a welcome new addition to the parks of New York City. Taking up a few acres, the park is gracefully landscaped with trees and flower beds. In the summer, it's overrun by office workers from the surrounding stock brokerages (although for some, the crowds do not impede romance), but, in the morning or early evening, you'll have a bench under the trees all to yourselves. This is a great place to rendezvous before dinner at one of the many restaurants in Tribeca. It is a rare, shimmering, sunny space in the city, enjoy it while it lasts. (**Note:** Open all year from approximately 8 a.m. to dusk.)

QUEENS BOTANICAL GARDEN
43-50 Main Street Flushing, Queens
(718) 886-3800

Take the Long Island Expressway westbound to Exit 23 (Main Street). Turn right at the light after you exit; this will put you onto Main Street. The street will dead end at the Garden's fence. Follow this around to your left till you reach Dahlia Avenue, the gate into the Garden.

Queens Botanical Garden packs a remarkable amount into its 39 sublime acres. In addition to its Rose Garden, which is the largest in the Northeast, the Garden is home to a series of individual pocket gardens, including a rock garden, a backyard garden, an herb garden and even a bee garden, all perfect places to spend an uninterrupted afternoon. Walkways lead past statues, a fountain encircled with tulips and a multitude of fragrant flower beds. The sundial near the entrance bears an appropriate message engraved on its face: *"Grow old with me, the best is yet to be."*

It's all quite serene, but I'm not being totally honest about what attracts us to this place — actually it is the chance to survey the Wedding Garden and daydream. Entrance is permitted only to private parties who rent the space, but you can peer through the picket fence and see everything. The Victorian era is evoked with a gazebo, a wooden chair swing and flowing willow shade trees. A brook meanders under a small foot bridge, feeding the exotic goldfish-stocked pond. Can you imagine 100 friends and relatives milling around here just for your special occasion?

Note: Main Street Flushing has become one of New York City's greatest melting pots. Be sure to walk the few blocks from the Garden and allow time to savor the Indian spice shops, browse through Chinese groceries and perhaps stop for an Afghan or Japanese lunch. The best stuff is sometimes just off Main Street, and so detours are encouraged.

RIVERSIDE PARK

The park borders the Hudson River to the west of Riverside Drive from 72nd Street to 145th Street.

Longer than Central Park, closer to what nature had originally intended and with a more dramatic setting, Riverside Park is often overlooked by those searching for a place to stroll. This park is actually a superb option for a romantic hour, simply because it is less popular and hectic than its more famous neighbor; and if you're coming from Broadway, you're closer to Riverside, anyway. This area is prime territory for leisure time together, away from the madding crowd. The towering trees and hilly meadows form the right setting for a relaxing country afternoon a few minutes from the very epitome of civilization. Aside from having spectacular vistas, the park is also dotted with monuments to local and far-flung heroes, from Ulysses

Grant to Joan of Arc. The generous use of marble, perhaps, gives the park a Parisian air.

♦ **Romantic Option:** If you'd like to cater yourself a scrumptious picnic, stop in at **Zabar's, Broadway at 80th Street, (212) 787-2000,** before you set out. From there, it's about a minute's walk to this unexpected acreage. You can also rent bicycles and make touring the park a swifter process.

♦ **Second Romantic Option: 79th Street Boat Basin,** *at 79th Street on the Hudson River,* is one of the great projects of builder Robert Moses and is an ideal locale for pretending to escape to an island getaway and a simpler way of life, even if just for a moment or two. The 125-slip marina, on the western edge of Riverside Park, is the year-round home of some 150 people, whose houseboats range in size and design from simple to grandiose. Sit awhile on a tree-shaded bench watching the boats rock gently in the water and feel the cool relief of Hudson River breezes. Come down on an early summer evening to see the sun set over the New Jersey Palisades. Barges and sailboats float by regularly and low-flying private planes pass overhead while the sea gulls drift by in the distance.

♦ **Romantic Warning:** If you don't know your way around the city, I'd call it a day with Grant's Tomb. It's probably not rewarding to venture beyond 125th Street. If you exit the park there, the Morningside Heights neighborhood can provide you with shops, bookstores, restaurants and some nice walks of its own.

SHORE ROAD WALK IN BAY RIDGE, Brooklyn ◆◗◆◗◆◗◆

Take the Brooklyn Bridge to the Brooklyn-Queens Expressway (278) south to Bay Ridge. Exit at Bay Ridge Parkway heading east. The road dead ends at Shore Road.

This is one of the most beautiful walks in the city. Shore Road snakes around the entire western edge of Bay Ridge. This small corner of Brooklyn is blessed by a majestic 180-degree view of the Narrows,

Verrazano Bridge, Staten Island and the land beyond. The area and view is so perfect it can easily motivate avid feelings of the heart.

As you follow the shoreline, you will notice large grassy areas, playgrounds, playfields and more grassy areas that seem to go on forever and forever. Somewhere here is your private area of the world from which to sit and watch the sun make its daily exit.

SNUG HARBOR, Staten Island
1000 Richmond Terrace
(718) 273-4477, 273-2060

From the Brooklyn-Queens Expressway, take the Verrazano Bridge to the Staten Island Expressway (Route 278) to the Clove Road Exit. Turn right on Clove Road and go about a mile to Bard Avenue, and make a sharp right onto it. Go several miles to the end of Bard Avenue, and then turn right onto Richmond Terrace. On your right you will see the entrance to Snug Harbor Cultural Center.

Snug Harbor is very appropriately named. An excursion to this fetching cultural center with its lush setting is a peaceful contrast to Manhattan business and nightlife. The Center is an 80-acre complex with Greek Revival buildings that are about 150 years old and are being restored. Originally a haven for sailors, the area now houses museums and theatres. There you can wander through the botanic gardens, nuzzle close in the gazebo or relax on the grounds near the duck pond.

On the grounds is a charming art museum called the Newhouse Gallery, which exhibits contemporary paintings and sculpture (it's open daily from 12 p.m. to 5 p.m. except Monday and Tuesday; admission is free). Despite its small size, it is international in scope and shows the work of well-known artists. The center also offers a wide range of entertainment: plays, films, dance, and musical concerts, some featuring top-name performers. I'll always treasure the memory of the balmy summer evening we spent there under the stars listening to the lilting voice of Judy Collins.

◆ *Romantic Suggestion:* To top off a day spent at Snug Harbor you can dine at **R.H. Tugs, 1115 Richmond Terrace, (718) 447-6369** (Moderate), a waterfront restaurant across the street from the harbor. Although decorated with tin ceilings and whirling fans, its main romantic appeal is the water, aglow with shimmering lights in the evening. Moon beams bouncing off the water's surface are hypnotically entrancing. Processions of tugboats will entertain you as they make their way across the Kill Van Kull. It is worth waiting for a table by the window. The cozy bar is as inviting as the restaurant. In warm weather you can get even closer to the water; drinks, hors d'oeuvres and barbecued dishes are served on the patio, where there is more privacy and the rhythmic sounds of the gulls and water becalm you. By the way, the food at Tugs is outstanding. Be sure not to miss the Tug Boat ice cream pie.

WAVE HILL, Bronx
Independence Avenue and 249th Street
(212) 549-2055

Take the Henry Hudson Parkway northbound to the 246th-250th Streets Exit or southbound to the 254th Street Exit. Follow the signs to the entry gate, which is two blocks west of the Parkway.

In late March when Midtown Manhattan hints only uncertainly of spring, Riverdale's Wave Hill estate, a mere fifteen minutes' drive north, is already munificent with the pleasures of the season. The verdant grounds overlook the Hudson glistening in the welcome sunshine, and the stately Palisades spread before you in the distance. Hundreds of trees, representative of the earth's far corners, are budding while purple *"Glory of the Snow"* festoon the hillsides. Workers tend the young gardens, which promise more delight in the months ahead when ripe herbs will diffuse their heady perfumes and exotic flowers will exhibit a riot of color. Even now the greenhouse is radiant with cacti in bloom, delicate orchids and calendulas of startling yellow and orange.

Built more than 150 years ago for attorney William Morris, Wave Hill House has seen a succession of notables in residence. Donated to the city in 1960, the estate is now the setting for a variety of cultural offerings. Art and photography exhibits fill the mansion's galleries and outdoor dance performances highlight the summer schedule. The auditorium, with its hand-carved ceilings, armor collection and panoramic river view makes a distinguished backdrop for Sunday afternoon chamber music concerts. Call for a calendar of events. Or come up on the spur of the moment for nature's ongoing spectacles staged in the fragrant air about you. On the woodland trails and rolling meadows, settle back, hold hands and let the birds and butterflies go on with the show.

> "LIFE IS JUST ONE FOOL THING AFTER ANOTHER;
> LOVE IS JUST TWO FOOL THINGS AFTER EACH OTHER."
>
> *Anonymous*

♦ Miscellaneous Kissing ♦

AFTERNOON TEA at the PARK LANE HOTEL
36 Central Park South *near 5th Avenue*
371-4000
Inexpensive

Most tearooms are too replete with women shoppers taking an afternoon break from Bloomingdale's to be considered even vaguely romantic. The Gold Room at the Helmsley Palace is one of the most entrancing tearooms I've ever seen, except that at teatime every table is female and a stray couple would be, at best, out of place; the atmosphere is far too distracting to qualify as an intimate place for a midday rendezvous. The Afternoon Tea at the Park Lane Hotel, on the other hand, is the antithetical environment to its counterpart at the Helmsley Palace and, for you, that is a romantic plus. It is truly the perfect place to be together at a time of day when most Americans are too busy to relax.

The large mahogany furnished room, covered in a thick, red, plush carpeting with a vast window regally overlooking Central Park, has a refined British atmosphere that is comfortable without being stuffy. Although this tearoom may not be as remarkable as the Gold Room, what it lacks in grandeur it makes up for with a stellar view of the park, a fabulous salmon and caviar tray and the richest pastries I've tasted anywhere. The entire meal only costs $12.50, or a la carte for around $7.00. This is an afternoon affair almost every budget can afford.

♦ *Romantic Warning & Suggestion:* I've been told that lunch here can be awful and the waiters inconsiderate. They must make a transformation at teatime, so give it a try. If not, then, as I said above, the very popular, very exquisite **Helmsley Palace's Gold Room, 455 Madison, 888-7000** (Moderate), one of the most opulent, grand places to have afternoon tea that I can think of, is worth the risk that you'll be one of the only male/female couples in the room.

CAVIARTERIA — See Petrossian Room (Restaurants French)

F.A.O. SCHWARZ TOY STORE
745 5th Avenue *at 58th Street*
644-9400

F.A.O. Schwarz is not a place for just anyone. You have to have a strong yearning to wander among rows and rows of adorable, multi-sized, snuggly stuffed animals, a need to play with toys, computerized and otherwise, frivolous or serious, and a will to be about six, seven, eight or nine for at least an hour or two. This maze of a toy store is for those couples who really know how to have fun and laugh out loud, the way you did when you were children and your parents let you loose at a carnival or in a toy store. Actually, it's a shame F.A.O. Schwarz doesn't have hours exclusively for big children like us. (I wrote the management a letter suggesting that but they haven't responded yet; it must be their nap time.)

What makes any of that romantic? Well, if you have to ask, then don't bother with this selection and go on to the others, instead. For those who know what I'm talking about, enjoy!

THE GRAND CENTRAL CATWALK

Enter this palatial structure from Vanderbilt Avenue and 44th Street. Behind the late-19th-century Commuter Bistro, which is on your left as you come in, you will find an elevator that will take you to the catwalk entrance on the top floor.

My husband insisted I include this one. He thought it was a wonderful and welcome change of pace from the usual things people do in New York. Well, he's right about that, but it's not often he finds something so thoroughly romantic as this; so, before you scoff, let me explain. Four stories over the amphitheatre-like waiting room of Grand Central Station, there is an old catwalk that spans the width of the building. Nowadays, it is hardly used (except by people like me and my husband) even though it provides an unusual perspective on one of New York's most outstanding pieces of architecture. Out in the middle of the walk, romantically inclined couples will literally feel like they are floating on air or suspended in space, high above the constellations twinkling against the pale blue ceiling of Grand Central. Below — as if you were riding in a balloon — arriving and departing passengers pace the marble floor oblivious of your quiet, awesome interlude. It is really a sight to behold.

There is one more location in here that is worth knowing about: Just outside of the famous Oyster Bar (many people tell me they find romantic) is a set of arches where you can actually throw your voice (sending verbal kisses) to each other. If you stand in diagonally opposite corners and whisper your endearments into the wall, your voice will carry across the ceiling to your mate, who will be the only one able to hear you.

A HANSOM CAB RIDE THROUGH CENTRAL PARK

The hansom cabs are parked along Central Park South between 5th and 7th Avenues.

Prior to this book assignment there was no way you would ever catch me doing anything as passe or as cinematically cliched as taking a buggy ride through Central Park. I remember doing it years ago and, well, it was stupid, and I had a bumpy, embarrassing time. When I started researching this book, I told my husband that when he came to New York I was saving this particular entry for him. I wanted to experience firsthand if time had changed my perceptions. Then there would be no question if the ride was romantic or, as I suspected, ridiculous.

On an early clear March morning, with the brisk air swirling around us and the sun warming our faces, we briefly discussed prices with our coachman. The only thing we wanted for our money was a romantic excursion, nothing more and nothing less. We climbed into the cab and cuddled under the heavy wool blanket, then realized we were both laughing. That's never a bad start. As the park opened up before us and the sounds of the city quieted, we found ourselves being lulled by the clip-clop of the horse's hooves striking the ground. The sun streamed through the trees and we continued laughing and talking and cuddling. About twenty minutes into the ride my husband nudged me and said, *"I don't know about you, but this is pretty good."* I snuggled a little closer and said, *"I know; don't rub it in."* All right, so I was wrong. Although it still seems a fairly touristy thing to do, there are certain things that change with time, even cliches, and what seemed silly back when, is often engaging today. Of course, it doesn't hurt to have a willing partner with a loving attitude for the excursion.

Note: The art of bartering with a hansom cab driver can be part of the whole escapade. As a rule, do not expect a bargain on a Friday or Saturday night when the weather is clear, warm and beautiful. On the other hand if there are several cabbies hanging around talking to each other — that's the drivers, not the horses — then you can give bargain-hunting your best shot.

LIMOUSINE SERVICE

Any special event or anything you choose to do in New York City can be done and done in style if you do it by limousine. The sheer number of car services in the yellow pages is probably unprecedented. What makes being chauffeur-driven romantic? New Yorkers don't have to ask, they already know!

MUSEUM KISSING

W hat can I say? The objects of beauty, history, creativity and majesty existing in the museums of New York City can evoke such emotion that if you don't have a significant other with you to embrace, you are likely to kiss a security guard. It is best then to not come alone. All the feelings you can imagine, and some you haven't thought of yet, are possible in this setting. And believe me, once is not enough. If the two of you are art lovers, you'll find ecstasy in many of the museums. It is likely that you will never see everything; for one thing, by the time you get through a whole museum, one or more of the exhibits will have changed and you'll have to start all over again. There are worse things.

American Museum of the Moving Image
35th Avenue *at 36th Street (for directions call (718) 784-4777)*
(718) 784-0077

What this museum lacks in convenience it makes up for in love and dedication to film and television, particularly the cinema. For those who are passionate about Greta Garbo, Alan Ladd, Cecile B. De Mille, D.W. Griffith, Marilyn Monroe, Jimmy Stewart and the history of Hollywood in general — this place is paradise. The exhibits are interesting and fun. Many allow the two of you to participate, but the real highlight is that your $5 ticket will let you see an entire day of films. Lights! Camera! Action!

Frick Collection
1 East 70th Street *at 5th Avenue*
288-0700

I wish the handful of estate museums near and on 5th Avenue didn't get so crowded, because they are truly bastions of heritage, priceless beauty and rapturous sights for the senses and soul. The

Frick collection is one of our favorites. The house is remarkable and the art is very European, with oversized portraits from Van Dyck and Whistler that are rare in most other art collections. Sharing this kind of beauty and resting awhile in the interior, glass-ceiling courtyard will guarantee a heart-stirring outing, regardless of the presence of others around you.

The Metropolitan Museum of Art
5th Avenue at 82nd Street
535-7710

Don't let the noisy, casually clad bodies sitting on the steps or in the entrance distract you from an incomparable romantic stroll. This place is not only magnificent but huge, taking up over four city blocks on four separate floors. Be assured that the bodies thin out as you proceed on to the various galleries. When you get to the less well known exhibits you will have left the crowds far behind. After you've wandered through several of the hidden wings and observed the display of colors and design that have spanned the centuries, be sure to visit the American Garden Court, one of the most comfortable and beautiful areas in the museum — or in the city, for that matter. You can sit and discuss your impressions in this spacious, glass-enclosed courtyard replete with wrought-iron benches, trees, works of art and a surrounding balcony.

The Museum of Broadcasting
1 East 53rd *at 5th Avenue*
752-7684

Similar to the American Museum of the Moving Image described above, this museum is dedicated exclusively to radio and television. If the two of you have ever spent an evening in couch potato heaven, then this outing is a fun, dedicated tribute to those hours of inter-twined bodies in front of the tube — only this time you can't fall asleep, which, of course, is to your courting advantage. The exhibits are thorough and the viewing rooms are very popular because they show lots of vintage television. Go during the week when it's less crowded, and the earlier the better.

Museum of Modern Art
11 West 53rd Street *between 5th & 6th Avenues*
708-9480

More often than not I don't understand modern art. I find it either absurdly depressing, confusing, strange, bizarre or silly or all five; which is probably what the artist intended me to feel in the first place. My husband is even worse, he feels that Picasso needed glasses and that Jackson Pollack tripped over a can of paint and started a new art form. Well, so much for us. For you, if you appreciate the unrivaled display of post-impressionistic art then there is no other place on earth quite like the Museum of Modern Art. Regardless of how you feel toward modern motifs, you can laugh or discuss it over coffee in the wondrous, easy-to-enjoy Sculpture Garden. The sculpture may not be easy to understand, but the loveliness of the garden is something the two of you will agree on wholeheartedly. *(Editor's Comment:* Excuse the interruption, but this contributor and I disagree on the intrinsic romantic value of modern art. What can be more blissful than gazing together at Van Gogh's original *Starry Night* having spent four years in college gazing at the poster of it on our dorm wall? Ah well, *de gustibus non es disputandum* — in matters of taste, there can be no dispute.)

PIER 17 at the SOUTH STREET SEAPORT
89 South Street *at Fulton Street*

I know, this one is probably a bit too popular for most romantic tastes. After all, the Pier is little more than a renovated shopping mall, much like shopping malls all over this country. But the view, oh that idyllic, calming, aquatic ring-side view of the city is, well, perfect, and on a sunny day, on weekends or bright evenings during any season, everyone else in the city seems to know that, too. What you can do is find the romance in the off hours or when the weather isn't to everyone else's liking. A foggy day can showcase the skyline in a slightly opaque, mysterious cover that you will probably be able to enjoy in relative seclusion. Or you can risk approaching the area on a balmy day or evening, past the cobblestoned, cafe-lined Fulton Street, which will be overflowing with energized, anxious singles seeking companions. If you've already found yours, I guess the carnival flavor can be exhilarating, plus you can skip the anxious search of those around you.

Pier 17 is a multilevel panoply of shops and restaurants overlooking the East River. There's a selection of upscale watering-holes facing all directions, each vying for the most glorious panorama. From the bar or the terrace of **Harbour Lights, 227-2800** (Expensive), three gleaming bridges highlight the Uptown landscape. Opposite, beyond the handsome interior of **Flutie's, 693-0777** (Expensive), rests an impressive array of sailing vessels. As you sip drinks in the water-borne breezes, the feel is more like a Mediterranean outpost than the hyper-financial whirl across the road.

There is a potentially amorous spirit to be found over dinner at **Sgarlato's Cafe, 619-5226** (Moderate), where you can admire the vista over casual fare in a cafe setting, or at the **Jade Sea Restaurant, 285-0505** (Moderate to Expensive), where tangy fresh sauces and traditional dishes are served with the same exquisite backdrop.

You can also take one of the many cruises that leave the Seaport most evenings during the warmer months. Call 608-9840 for the schedule. The cruise won't float much beyond lower Manhattan, but the sunset views of the Statue of Liberty and the skyscrapers along the shore are exquisite. The rock 'n' roll cruise is particularly festive. A band plays the perennial soul favorites for dancing, with the deck vibrating to the rhythm of two-stepping couples. By the time you dock, it's New Year's Eve again; sing, sway, kiss and hug to your hearts' content.

Romantic Note: Most all of the restaurants at Pier 17 offer nighttime entertainment. This is just one special, vibrant face of the Seaport. If it sounds like an excess of gaiety, remember, visit in the off hours or during inclement weather. The beauty can still be relished but with more cordial, quiet delight.

Second Romantic Note: In the summer months, almost all of the restaurants at the Pier offer Sunday brunch with terrace seating. If you can get through the crowds or arrive early (10 a.m.), it is truly a wonderful place to start summer mornings off on the right soothing note.

One More Romantic Note: Just off of Fulton Street, in a small garden court area, well hidden from the bustling crowd, is **McDuffy's, 619-8092** (Inexpensive), a small, very intimate bar with a handful of tables and no standing room to speak of. There's also no entertainment or view except the two of you gazing into each other's eyes. That can be more than enough entertainment for some.

◆ *Possible Romantic Option:* **Caroline's, 233-4900** (Expensive), at the Seaport, is a well-known nightspot that features some of the best comedy this town has to offer as you dine on very decent seafood and Continental cuisine. It may not be romantic, but it's definitely fun, and fun can be a nice accent to almost anything else you choose to do together.

RICHMONDTOWN RESTORATION, Staten Island
441 Clark Avenue
(718) 351-1617

From the Verrazano-Narrows Bridge follow the signs for New Jersey west to Richmond Road/Clove Road Exit, turning left at the second traffic light after you exit onto Richmond Road. About five miles ahead, turn left onto St. Patrick's Place and follow signs to Richmondtown Parking.

Think of this as Williamsburg North. In the middle of Staten Island, you can explore the colonial way of life by wandering through the inviting grounds and well-preserved buildings of this unexpected historical oasis. Nestle by the pond and feed the ducks, watch demonstrations of old-fashioned crafts by costumed artisans or go on a guided tour inside the 14 handsomely restored buildings. Traveling to a restoration may sound like an academic exercise; yet, each time we stroll from the parking lot to the recreated village, we know every step draws us into a bygone era, and our fantasies and imaginations are fueled for a long time to come.

At Richmondtown, everything is people-oriented, rather than technology-centered. Sensual pleasures include the smell of bread baking in colonial brick ovens, richly detailed handmade furniture and a gentle landscape that encourages meandering. You can even learn 18th- and 19th-century ballroom dance or hearthside cooking, and you can attend a quilting bee. For us, the most romantic events are the Friday and Saturday night concerts in the candlelit tavern, presenting folk music of the period in a rustic setting. You'll want to snuggle close on the wooden benches and enjoy the music. In winter, a very real fireplace creates authentic warmth for both shows. To stay in the Early American frame of mind, have dinner before or a snack after the concert at **M. Bennett's Restaurant, (718) 979-5258** a colonial bistro next door to the tavern. The tavern and restaurant are small, so reservations are a must and the concerts are seasonal ending sometime in June and starting again in the fall.

Note: Admission price is included in the cost of the concert tickets.

SCHIRMER MUSIC
61 West 62nd Street *at Columbus Avenue*
541-6236

Whether it be the Beatles, Beethoven, Van Halen, Sondheim, Billy Ocean or The New York Philharmonic playing Mel Torme favorites, you will find it somewhere in Schirmer's, the sheet-music lover's paradise. If you've ever said to each other, *"They're playing our song,"* then at some point it will require the melodious tones of your own voices to do it justice. What better way to celebrate any romantic occasion than with a personal rendition of a special tune to your beloved.

SKATE-A-DATE — See American Festival Cafe (Restaurants American)

> "IT JUST TAKES AN ATTITUDE CHANGE TO TURN
> THE DELIRIUM INTO DELIGHT."
>
> *Me*

WORTH THE TRIP

♦ Long Island ♦

Note:The descriptions that follow are loosely arranged from west to east heading away from Manhattan.

Traveling to Long Island is an unconditional romantic must, because, to put it simply, there is everything here two people in love could want to share. Part of the Island is a series of cosmopolitan towns that feed directly into New York City. As the miles take you further east, most memories of modern civilization are left far behind. This is one huge land mass, resplendent with forest, quaint fishing villages, miles upon miles of winding roads, sandy white beaches, explosive ocean surf, rustic lodges, quaint bed & breakfasts and acre after acre of very exclusive, prime East Coast real estate.

Narrowing down the entries for Long Island's best kissing places was a struggle because so much of this area is distinctively beautiful and interesting. The variety of terrain and culture may make it difficult for you to decide where to go first. The North and the South Shores have very different characters, but which one to visit will often come down to a coin toss. One thing is clear though: for either a day trip, a long lazy weekend or a lengthy stay, Long Island is a sensible, romantic, New York place to holiday any time of the year.

ROSLYN and the ROSLYN DUCK POND

*Twenty miles northeast of Manhattan. Take the Long Island Expressway
(I405) to Exit 37 north. Once on the service road, pass Willis Avenue
and proceed to Roslyn Road, where you'll turn left. This becomes Main
Street. Watch for the signs indicating Roslyn Park that will direct you
through the village center and straight to the Duck Pond.*

Well-known and dutifully visited for generations, the Roslyn Duck
Pond somehow has retained a serenity that will have you falling in
love all over again. I was first here about 30 years ago when Roslyn
was far less developed and there were not quite as many ducks (I
guess they have come to find it romantic too), but surprisingly, the
town feels even more pristine and lovely than I remember. The
handsome rolling lawn is nibbled neat and trim by resident aquatic
birds who often provide great natural entertainment. There is plenty
of room for couples to wander in, a 1774 paper mill to amble through
and a small bandstand pagoda and wooden footbridge spanning the
channeled stream that leads to the three levels of the pond, before
you reach Hempstead Harbor on the outskirts of town.

The park is in a valley nestled between two well-timbered hills; in
the valley, stone dwellings dating to 1690 neighbor inspired contemporary homes. All of Roslyn is steeped in history and a stroll through
the town's park can help unburden your thoughts so that you can
dwell on the matter at hand; to wit, each other. The town itself is
as entrancing as it was years ago and Main Street has a handful of
dining options to allow time for a brief respite from your journey.

♦ *Romantic Warning:* There are benches and picnic tables at the
Duck Pond, but even more plentiful are trees to shelter you from the
sun and heat. However, beware of territorial geese that have been
known to try and claim their land back from those visiting their part
of the world. And, although no dogs are allowed in the park, the
birds themselves contribute noticeable enrichment to the soil. That's
probably why everything is so green, but watch where you sit and walk.

♦ *Romantic Option:* A very lovely afternoon can be spent at the

Nassau County Fine Arts Center, which features a **Museum of Fine Arts** and the **William Cullen Bryant Preserve**. The Center/Museum is located just to the east and north of Roslyn, off Northern Boulevard (Route 25A). Here, find the **Frick Estate**, a Georgian mansion with art galleries and 145 acres of well-manicured lawns, meadows, ponds and glens. The grounds are also home to outdoor sculpture and formal gardens, but what is most remarkable about the site is that it has retained the character of perpetual leisure that the landed gentry so enjoyed in a more loving, less hasty time.

THE CHALET, Roslyn
One Railroad Avenue
(516) 621-7975
Moderate

Twenty miles northeast from Manhattan, take the Long Island Expressway to Exit 37. Once on the service road, pass Willis Avenue. Proceed to Roslyn Road and turn left. In less than 1.5 miles, turn left immediately after passing under the railroad bridge. The restaurant is a few yards up the hill on the right.

Not many restaurants have it all. The Chalet comes close. Its greatest virtue is its intimate warmth. Unaffected and unpretentious and set on a wooded hillside, the Chalet has a deserved reputation as that rare dining spot with food, service, decor and location that add up to a desirable evening out. The Chalet's building is a storybook creation, dating from the 1800s, of stone and brick with gingerbread-like details. Inside is an uncluttered Victorian interior of mirrors, quilts, hanging antiques and bentwood chairs. In warmer months, the second-floor outdoor balcony opens to extra seating for dining under the trees and stars, and out here there are plenty of both. The Chalet is not fancy, but the elements meld, surpassing all of your out-of-town romantic expectations.

The service is attentive — which means they attend to your privacy as well as your dining; they're friendly without being intrusive. Classical or light jazz background music adds nicely to your sentimental feelings. The menu offers the familiar, blended tastefully with the imaginative; a recent appetizer of smoked venison sausage slices, with a spicy black bean sauce topped by red peppers, scallions and sour cream, was fabulous. You may be tempted to try one or many of the other restaurants in Roslyn and nearby. Some are better decorated. Some are quite famous and expensive and a number boast historical locations or harbor views; but none except the Chalet treats your heart as well.

♦ **Romantic Option:** After dinner, walk through the historic preservation district of Roslyn, down the hill and past the Roslyn Duck Ponds to window-shop and have a drink at the **George Washington Manor, 1305 Old Northern Boulevard, (516) 621-1200** (the 1753 Onderdonk House where George really did spend the night). There you can tarry most romantically on the truly sublime outdoor patio, which features yet another Roslyn Pond.

OLD WESTBURY GARDENS
Old Westbury Road
(516) 333-0048

Take the Long Island Expressway to Glen Cove Road (Exit 39 south). Follow the service road eastbound, 1.2 miles. Turn right onto Old Westbury Road. Continue one-quarter mile to the Gardens.

"Let's take some time to smell the roses," urged my mate, reminding us we needed respite from workaholic New York City life. He knew just the place for restoration: Old Westbury Gardens. This hundred-acre haven is a typical English country estate, plunked improbably in the middle of Nassau County. And lucky for us! At Old Westbury, we not only smelled the roses, but reveled in the scent and sensation of walking through the woods on a carpet of pine needles while watching the swans glide on the lake and fat geese waddle on the

thick emerald lawns. There's a grove of wooden tables in this sylvan setting for bring-your-own picnics. For the less prepared a snack bar provides light fare.

Built at the turn of the century as a private residence, the Gardens are home to a stately mansion surrounded by sculpted gardens and woodlands. The interior of the house, with its 18th-century antiques and fine paintings by Gainsborough, Constable, Sargent and others, is well worth the tour. But the grounds and walkways dotted with benches twixt the floral profusion all around is the romantic part. You can sit on the benches at the Temple of Love, among its fluted stone columns beneath a lacy wrought-iron canopy, and gaze like we did at the swans and ducks on the lake.

Note: The Gardens are open Wednesday through Sunday, from late April through October. There is also a series of Picnic Pops Concerts during these months, beginning at 7 p.m. for a charge of $6.00.

PLANTING FIELDS ARBORETUM

From New York City take the Long Island Expressway to Exit 39 north (Glen Cove Road). Go north on Glen Cove Road to 25A (Northern Boulevard). Turn right, heading east on 25A. Turn left (north) onto Wolver Hollow Road. At the end, turn right onto Chicken Valley Road. The entrance to the Arboretum is in about one mile, on the right.

This just may be the most romantic place you'll ever see. Your first reaction will be to call this vast acreage a park, albeit an idyllic park, but it's not really a park at all; it is the former baronial estate of a man named Coe. What makes it so sublime is the picture-perfect setting of the landscape. You enter through wrought-iron gates and from there the trails are surrounded by green willow trees, sprawling hardwood trees, shrubs of every imaginable variety, glorious fountains, and rolling hills where displays of radiant native and exotic flowers cover the area in a kaleidoscope of colors. This is an unparalleled collection of the best mother nature has to offer. It is so large that it is almost impossible not to feel totally alone here, even at the height of the summer.

The winter months may send snowy blasts across their windows, but the greenhouses at the Planting Fields are a world where the mysteries of color and life do not cease, like a giant, lush Garden of Eden. The fragrant orchids and lilies, the Camellia House, in bloom from December to mid March, and the other greenhouses with their high, sparkling glass windows, and walls covered in moss and vine, are spellbinding. Every turn of the head will bring something beautiful into view.

The mansion itself, Coe Hall, one of the nation's finest, has special events. Call first to find out what is taking place, (516) 922-0479. As a dear friend once told me, I wouldn't go out with anyone who wouldn't take me to the Planting Fields for a date. I can see why she feels that way.

Note: There is a minimal admission of $1.50 per person.

SEA CLIFF

From either the Long Island Expressway or Northern State Parkway, take the Glen Cove Road exit north. Continue on Glen Cove Road past 25A (Northern Boulevard) for about another five miles until you see the Sea Cliff sign. Bear right there and make an immediate left (at the first light) onto Sea Cliff Avenue. Follow this for a little over two miles — up the hill, beyond the Long Island Railroad tracks into the town itself.

Sea Cliff is a town where the atmosphere is deepened by time and generations of life around the same hearths and small town. It is a place for walking, replete with many small, intimate streets. There is something wonderful at every turn — flowers tumbling over wooden fences, wildflower gardens, and the views, the ocean breeze and taste of salt on your lips.

Stop in the town for a leisurely afternoon of browsing and antique shopping along Sea Cliff Avenue. You can have lunch at **Once Upon a Moose, corner of Sea Cliff Avenue and Central Avenue,**

(516) 676-9304 (Inexpensive), or, kitty-cornered from it, load up for your picnic at **Arata's, (516) 671-0290,** and head off for the beach. You could stop at **Prospect Park** at the end of town. It's known for spectacular views of the harbor and the Connecticut shoreline in the distance, and unsurpassed sunsets where the blaze of the passing day sets the water on fire. Or turn right on Prospect and then left down the hill on Cliff Way, all the while overlooking the water, to the benches of **Sea Cliff Park** — just a few feet from the shoreline.

COLD SPRING HARBOR

(Not to be confused with Cold Spring, New York.) Follow the directions to Sea Cliff, then drive south on Sea Cliff Avenue to the end, making a short right and left onto Glen Cove Road. This will take you to 25A (Northern Boulevard). Turn east for thirteen miles from the Glen Cove intersection where 25A descends toward the waters of Cold Spring Harbor.

Five different people told me not to forget to mention the town of Cold Spring Harbor. I was told the drive itself was a wonderful excursion into the country and into a world of serenity and beauty. As you head east you drive past fine old houses, woods, nurseries, horse farms, winding road and endless countryside. The town itself, or rather Main Street, is a small-shop-browser's heaven. Romantic is a wide word, but within it has to be a street where many of the houses were built during the prime of an 1850s whaling boom. The harbor is the frame for the entire setting and it gives an aura of languid, wondrous beauty. Of course, aside from filling your souls with the sights and sounds of this town and cruising through the delightful crafts, antiques and crystal shops, there is a certain romance to stopping in at Merrill Lynch Realty and laying hands on some of this fabulous property, or at least thinking about it.

◆ *Romantic Suggestion:* **The Country Kitchen, 55 Main Street, Cold Spring Harbor, (516) 692-5655** (Inexpensive), has been a luncheon favorite for decades, and **The Old Whaler Restaurant,**

105 Harbor Road, Cold Spring Harbor, (516) 367-3166 (Moderate), across from the harbor, has withstood the test of years.

NORTHPORT

Follow the directions to Cold Spring Harbor. Another eight miles eastward on 25A (Northern Boulevard) will bring you to Northport. Make a left at Woodbine Road, which will bring you to the foot of Main Street.

On your way to Northport, if you're following your map, it is worthwhile to stop along the way at Huntington or Centerport, perhaps for some sightseeing at the planetarium or the Vanderbilt Estate. Otherwise, the scenic drive to Northport has some radiant visual pleasures of its own and, given that you can't do everything, one destination at a time is probably plenty. Cow Park is in the center of town on the harbor, where sailboats rest peacefully in the water. You can lounge on the grass and take in a summer concert at the gazebo.

To really put the glow on this excursion you need to go the extra mile(s) and drive past Main Street on Woodbine, past some truly exquisite beachside Victorian mansions, turning right up the James Street hill and left on Ocean Avenue to the end, where you head left and down to the village of **Asharoken.** Here is an extraordinary drive along a road separating the Long Island Sound from Huntington Bay — a breathtaking and tranquil stretch with beach houses and sea birds and cool ocean breezes. Drive on past the Coast Guard Station road and follow the signs to the beach. **Hobart Beach** is a sandy finger protecting a tiny harbor and pointing out between the bay and the sound. Shed your shoes and take that long rejuvenating walk amid the beach grasses and jetty boulders and finish out a rare, unspoiled day in relative privacy together in your own corner of the world.

THE JOHN PEEL ROOM at the ISLAND INN, Westbury
Old Country Road at Roosevelt Raceway
(516) 228-9500
Moderate to Expensive

Take the Long Island Expressway to Exit 38 heading south to the Northern State Parkway. Take Exit 31A heading south until you reach Old Country Road, turning east. The Inn will be on your right.

Brunch at the John Peel Room is a delightful way to transform an ordinary Sunday brunch into an enchanting Victorian dining experience. As you enter the large dining room, you will be greeted by the plaintive strumming of live harp music. The decor is warm and New England cozy, the high-back chairs are wide and comfortable and the paintings all about help to create the aura that is so inviting and so very romantic. In the middle of the first dining area are large floral centerpieces, and at the rear is an open hearth where one can see the diligent workings of the kitchen.

Before you even embark on your meal, you can sit in the lounge on cushy couches in front of a glowing fireplace. Once the meal begins, sit back and together watch the parade of pastries, fluffy gourmet omelets, giant apple pancakes with lingonberries, quiches and crepes being served courteously all around. Choosing is the only difficult part of being here. If you do nothing else (besides kiss in between courses) save room for dessert. If you are a chocolate lover the triple chocolate cake is irresistibly delectable.

♦ *Romantic Suggestion:* If you want to turn this morning event into an evening getaway, the adjoining Island Inn has many lovely rooms to choose from.

ROBERT MOSES STATE PARK

Almost fifty miles from Manhattan, using the Long Island Expressway (Interstate 405) to Exit 53, which is the Sagtikos Parkway, south to Robert Moses Causeway. Before reaching the Causeway, you will actually be on the westbound Southern State Parkway for about one mile; it will then intersect with the Causeway. Don't let this confuse you; just follow the signs.

For more than nine months of the year, the parking lots at Long Island's beaches — not to mention the beaches themselves — are virtually empty. Perhaps people don't realize that the ocean operates year round. It's to your romance's great advantage, though, that the masses seem to find surf and sand suitable only for swimming and sunning. Throughout the year, excepting those hot and beach-perfect days in July and August, and on occasion June, couples can find virtually complete privacy — for miles — under an enormous sky untouched by concrete and commercialism.

The approach to the park is a sight to behold. Three bridges, one an authentic drawbridge, must be crossed before reaching the entrance on the western end of Fire Island. On a clear day the view is vast. There is an abundance of everything restless surf lovers could want. The spectrum of blues ebb and flow into each other as the waves undulate on the horizon. The shoreline seems to go on forever and its creative uses are many: hunt for shells, walk along the water's edge, build castles, bury your feet in the cool damp sand or just sit and talk — or not, the ocean can speak for both of you most eloquently. Don't leave without taking it all in — the skittering birds, the salty fresh air, the constant, raging rhythm of the waves and the footprints you leave; they'll always be there, even after the waters and wind have washed over them. For a trip to the beach together is really a trip deep within yourselves.

Note: Robert Moses State Park is less well known, less developed and half the size (it covers a mere 1,000 acres) of the more popular Captree, Gilgo and Jones Beach State Parks, fifteen miles due west of here. Robert Moses State Park offers the same fine ocean sand, colorful shells and turbulent surf Long Island is famous for, but the fact that it is on rustic, roadless Fire Island lends this acreage a great deal of privacy. In fact, as most people who know of Robert Moses Park realize it is on Fire Island, they incorrectly assume it is accessible only by the seasonable passenger-only ferryboats that carry sun-worshippers to summer rentals. Of course, many ocean lovers choose to visit Jones Beach just because it is developed — that way there is more for the kids to do. But I understand that's not what you are looking for . . .

♦ *Romantic Option:* If somehow you tire of Robert Moses, you might want to visit **Tobay Beach Bird & Game Sanctuary**, which is nine miles west of the Causeway, on Ocean Parkway. It is located on the bay side and you can take a hike through salt marshland in a somewhat more secluded and composed setting.

BAYARD CUTTING ARBORETUM, Oakdale
Montauk Highway
(516) 581-1002

Fifty miles from Manhattan, using the Long Island Expressway (I405) to Exit 53 (Sagtikos Parkway) south, to Southern State Parkway east, to Exit 45E (Route 27A). The Arboretum is less than one mile beyond the exit ramp.

This oasis of beauty and quiet can feel like your own private retreat while you explore its carefully planned and meticulously maintained grounds. The area projects a European flavor with its setting on the cliffs of the pastoral Connetquot River, graceful shade trees rising from the banks of its mirrored surface and black-faced swans floating languidly by. There are plentiful, handsomely crafted wrought-iron benches overlooking all of it. There are six marked walks you may take, although you'll no doubt prefer to stroll about casually, turning here and there on any whim or impulse. Depending on the time of year, there will be fragrant, heavenly displays of flowers along the way.

◆ **Romantic Option:** A walk back in time correctly describes but does not even hint at the romance to be found on a visit to the **Mews in Oakdale**, a short drive from the Arboretum. Here you will find an unusual collection of quaint buildings that form a sort of walled village. This is a sweet haven of white picket fences, brick and gravel drives, copper pipes and flashings, cupolas, wishing wells and patiently tended gardens, all on shady one-way lanes. *To reach the Mews from the Arboretum, take 27A east to 27 east and stay right, exiting immediately at County Road 85 (Montauk Highway). At the first traffic light (Idlehour Boulevard), turn right. Continue about one mile to Hollywood Drive. The Tower Mews arch is just ahead. Park on Hollywood or Idlehour, no parking is allowed in the Mews.*

STONY BROOK

Sixty miles from Manhattan, using the Long Island Expressway (I495) to Exit 62 north (Nicolls Road) to left on 25A (westbound). Pass the LIRR station and turn right on Main Street. At this light, 25A continues to the right. Follow this into Stony Brook.

Stony Brook is one of a handful of villages on Long Island's North Shore that have evolved into a cozy blend of authentic rural, with all the historical details in place, and the highly sophisticated, which together conspire to sweep your hearts away. To take advantage of all the potential romance that abounds in these parts, living here is probably a prerequisite, but barring that dreamy possibility, you'd do well enough to meander through this village and the surrounding neighboring areas. It is all as enchanting as you could imagine.

Along Main Street is a jewel of a pond framed by wooded nesting areas and frequented by graceful swans. There is a timeless dewy feeling in this place. The Mill Pond which feeds the brook (the town's namesake) turns the water wheel of the adjacent mill (circa 1699). The brook leads into Stony Brook Harbor and to an expansive sandy beach, passing the Hercules figurehead salvaged from the *USS Ohio* (launched in 1820). Going the short distance from the pond to the beach, you'll pass terraced, ivy-covered walls, colonial houses and a handsome Federal-style business district. There is still a sleepy air in this part of the world; the ancient trees, secluded harbor, endless country setting and nearby ocean surf are responsible for this and will rouse a sweet, satisfied spirit of oneness.

♦ *Romantic Suggestion:* Be sure to walk up Harbor Road (between the Mill Pond and the Grist Mill itself) into the head of the harbor area. The hilly, winding roads lead past homes and farms set in rolling meadows and woods and thickets. From some spots, you can see the harbor and beyond to Smithtown Bay (in Long Island Sound). If you can walk at least as far as the breathtaking mansion on the hill, with its own idyllic pond (less than two miles on the right), you'll feel certain you're really in Switzerland.

♦ *Romantic Option:* Pick up delicious food for a picnic lunch or dine informally in the **Purple Plum, 1007 Route 25A, (516) 751-3250** (Inexpensive), a gourmet deli at the opposite end of Stony Brook. If the weather doesn't lend itself to outdoor eating, excellent dining with a splendid water view can be had at the **Three Village Inn, The Harborview** and **Stony Brook**; the **Mirabelle** has no view but it is one of the best restaurants to be found anywhere. (The aforementioned restaurants have their own listings in this section.)

♦ *Second Romantic Option:* **The John Christopher Gallery, 131 Main Street, (516) 689-1601,** is proof that a gift shop can provide a loving interlude. A browse through this shop is special not only for the quality craftworks beautifully displayed, but for the gentle and evocative music being played either by tape or sometimes by local virtuosos. Many of the stores here (which include designer names) call themselves "*Shoppes,*" but unlike many stores who give themselves this self-conscious appellation, the shoppes here in Stony Brook warrant the extra letters.

♦ *Romantic Warning:* Watch those "*no parking*" signs — they are strictly enforced. Also, note postings of private property. Trespassers are not tolerated.

THREE VILLAGE INN, Stony Brook
150 Main Street
(516) 751-0550
Inn: Moderate
Restaurant: Moderate to Expensive

Using the Long Island Expressway (I495) to Exit 56, take Route 111
north and follow the signs carefully, continuing to the end, where it runs
into Route 25A eastbound (at a large intersection in Smithtown). The Inn
is 1.5 miles farther down 25A.

Rambling and sedate, this positively charming inn dates back to
1751 and was the home of Long Island's first millionaire. Its country
colonial decor complements a natural maple floor and low-beamed
ceiling and it occupies a site very close to Stony Brook's harbor. The
rooms in the main building are quite pleasant and large; all have
private baths and look out onto lovely grounds. There are six private
cottages facing the water, some with fireplaces.

In the excellent restaurant, servers in appropriate colonial garb
offer fresh-baked breads and fresh, beautifully prepared seafood. A
fire is often roaring on cool evenings and on weekends a pianist adds
a few more sparks. The balmy harbor is visible from many tables in
this cozy location.

◆ *Romantic Option:* **The Harborview Restaurant, 93 Main**
Street, Stony Brook, (516) 689-7755 (Inexpensive), provides good
food in a cozy atmosphere and the price is as attractive as the location.

MIRABELLE, St. James
404 North Country Road (Route 25A)
(516) 584-5999
Expensive

1.1 miles west of Moriches Road and 25A junction. Just east of the light at the intersection of Edgewood, Woodlawn and 50 Acre Roads.

Mirabelle is that miracle of a dream come true: Classically trained French chef and savvy gourmet writer marry; they open an exquisite restaurant in a simple 19th-century farmhouse in the country, and they sate the palates and the spirits of fortunate, like-minded appetites. The owners here really know what they're doing, and what they do is quite remarkable. They create a romantic dining haven without relying on the appurtenances we usually think of as requisite for blissful eating. What they've done is kept the decor simple, elegant and understated. The staff is friendly but not familiar, formal but not stuffy. Wall sconces and votives in crystal holders provide subdued lighting; fresh flowers are in abundance and a large portion of the tables are set for two. In warm weather the outdoor terrace is a charming garden site for a drink, and although the restaurant is quite close to the road, its red gravel and brick walkways and casual landscape keep what's on the other side further away than would otherwise seem possible. What really makes the Mirabelle's heart tick is the food. We had a brilliant meal there, and we knew after finishing that we would return to this find again and again.

PORT JEFFERSON

*Sixty-five miles from Manhattan, using the Long Island Expressway (I495)
to Exit 63 heading north on County Road 83 (North Ocean Avenue, also
known as Patchogue-Mount Sinai Road). Turn left at the junction with
Route 112 five miles down the road, which eventually becomes Main Street
and Route 25A westbound and leads straight into town.*

Port Jefferson, first settled in 1682, was always a bustling harbor
community until just about a decade ago, when it became gentrified
and cosmopolitan and better known as an historic seaport. Now a
walk along Main Street, at times crowded with tourists during the
sun-soaked summer months but practically empty off season, takes
you into a beguiling harbor with views across the water to Connecticut. Even when you can't see quite that far across, the blue of Long
Island Sound is inspiring. You'll feel as if civilization had just washed
away and you were here alone with each other, away from it all. Your
city ears will hear mysterious sounds: those of your footsteps as you
walk on the dock's reverberating boards and the adrift-at-sea lull in
the slap of the water on the boats and moorings.

◆ *Romantic Suggestion:* As lunch-time approaches here, one
takes to wandering about town. Our favorite place to wander is
Moore's Gourmet Market, 225 Main Street, (516) 928-1443,
where we usually choose an exquisite picnic. Everything from caviar
to wickedly rich desserts is available. To enjoy your feast get back in
your car and drive about two miles west from the blinking light at
the foot of Main Street on 25A to Setauket, where there are at least
three glorious semi-rural spots to lay out a blanket away from everyone
and dine elegantly, alfresco. The spot we always head for is the beach
area in the Dyer's Neck Historic District.

◆ *Romantic Alternative:* If eating indoors is your preferred style
of dining then you can do that in superb style at **Danford's Inn at
Bayles Dock,** complete with a water view and fresh seafood. Or for
a tenderly romantic setting, **Savories** is best. (These places have their
own listings in this section.) For good food in a more casual atmos-

phere, **The Printer's Devil, 105 Wynne Lane, Port Jefferson, (516) 928-7171** (Reasonable), with its stained glass, rich oak detailing and contemporary accents, is a friendly, casual, publike dining alternative.

DANFORD'S INN, Port Jefferson
25 East Broadway
(516) 928-5200
Inn: Moderate
Restaurant: Moderate

Use the Long Island Expressway to Exit 63 (North Ocean Avenue) turning north (left) at the first light after you exit. Proceed to Route 112 turning left again. This will take you straight into Port Jefferson and will become Route 25A westbound as well as Main Street, which ends at the harbor where you make a right onto East Broadway. Danford's is a few yards further.

Imagine having your own balcony overlooking the harbor that takes in an unhindered water view. At dawn, dusk or midday the sun across Port Jefferson harbor will undoubtedly create the backdrop for one of the special moments of your stay here. Danford's rooms can give you all of that and more. The suites themselves, most of them recently built, are studiously designed in 18th- and 19th-century motifs which nicely overcome the sterile uniformity that newer constructions tend to project. Modern convenience is well blended with the abundant heritage at this inn and the restaurant and common areas all follow this tradition with great care and respect. The lobby is a warm and rich space with a crackling fireplace casting an amber glow all around. Speaking of fireplaces, a few suites and parlors have their own. In addition to the daily Continental breakfast, a hearty breakfast buffet is served on weekends.

The Danford's Inn restaurant doesn't overdo its nautical theme (which is appreciated) and it is lovely to dine on one of the glass-enclosed porches overlooking the harbor. Watch the ferryboat as it

docks, the sailboats tack across the water or just watch the water do
what it does best: instill lasting, comforting impressions and memories.
The mood here is comfortable but not overly casual. The interior
has a refreshingly bright air, even at night in the subdued light . . .
all very relaxing and very civilized and very satisfying.

SAVORIES, Port Jefferson
218 Wynne Lane
(516) 331-4747
Moderate to Expensive

*Follow the directions to Port Jefferson using Route 112. About one mile
after crossing the train tracks, Wynne Lane appears, where you then turn
left and proceed to the parking lot. Savories is adjacent to this lot.*

Savories resides on a quaintly nostalgic lane next to some appealing
pretty shops — white lace drapes across leaded and stained glass
windows with fan lights supplying light inside. A boardwalk wraps
around this large bay building, hugging a tall shade tree overlooking
a sweet little pond. (Beyond this is a fairly large parking lot, but
somehow it's hardly noticeable.)

Inside Continental meets continental. The European lace is
complemented by stately American colonial furnishings and exposed
brick walls. At night the rooms are dimly lit with only the vibrant
glow of candles flickering from each table. The menu is a hearty
selection of fish, lamb, duck and more all served with aplomb.
Table-side preparations are ongoing, the atmosphere chivalric and
the outcome superb. Anticipate a leisurely and formal but altogether
gracious dining experience.

◆ *Romantic Warning:* Savories is very Continental, to the point
that its menu speaks the language of the food; French fare is written
in French, Italian items in Italian and so on. We love reading and
speaking other languages, but that could just be us; others may find
it a bit like the one-day, three-country tour.

WILDWOOD STATE PARK, Wading River
North Country Road
(516) 929-4314

About 75 miles from Manhattan, using the Long Island Expressway (I495) to Exit 68 north (William Floyd Parkway) to Route 25A (Sound Avenue) east to Hulse Landing Road and then north to the park.

There are places to kiss and there are places you wish you could kiss in. On Long Island, many of the best places to kiss seem to be privately owned. Not so at Wildwood State Park. This is one of the few camping locations on the Island. In my opinion it's the only camping facility worth pitching a tent at. As for pitching woo, this can be done anywhere, but here at Wildwood it can be done with great effect, and a connection with nature is rare in these parts.

The park sits on Long Island Sound in the midst of acres serenely devoted to agricultural use. But the cultivated flat plain you cross as you approach and enter the park soon becomes well-treed and then thickly wooded as the land starts to roll with little hills and valleys. Suddenly, the land ends — a sheer bluff drops to the beach and a tranquil body of water laps at the shoreline. The steep paths to the beachfront are themselves glorious; through breaks in the trees as the two of you make your way down to the shore, you can see the watery horizon with birds in the thickets offering their songs.

The beach here is quite unique. In one large area, where one would expect to find sand, there is an immense track of pebbles, tumbled smooth and oval by the force of waves. Some boulders in the water are good perches when the tide is out. Camping is not on the beach but set back a little in the hills. Here there are some beautiful little secluded glens where you can set up camp.

♦ **Romantic Warning:** The first time we camped here, it was in very hot weather and we set up our tent without paying attention to orientation. In the morning we awakened with the southeastern sun turning our tent into a greenhouse. Plan ahead, or ask the rangers for their suggestions.

SAG HARBOR

About 100 miles from Manhattan, using the Long Island Expressway (I495) to Exit 70, head south on Route 111 to Route 27 east, which becomes Montauk Highway after Southampton, to Bridgehampton. Turn left onto County Road 79 (Bridgehampton-Sag Harbor Turnpike) at the War Monument Obelisk. This road leads directly into Sag Harbor.

There's an irony to the making of great romantic places. Take New York City and Sag Harbor, for instance. Two hundred years ago, the two were the fledgling United States' official ports of entry. Today they have, to say the least, nothing in common, except perhaps for well-deserved reputations (and some residents who maintain homes in each). Unlike the well-known, well-developed Hamptons on the South Shore of Long Island, which are on the water's edge, Sag Harbor has retained its intimate haven status mostly because it is a few miles farther inland. It is definitely off the beaten track and its tranquility and scenic beauty are transcendent. I can predict two things about your visit here: The two of you will fall irretrievably in love with this town and you'll be kissing with inspiration as well.

Romance abounds in Sag Harbor. There's a languid feel to the air, the stately lichen-covered trees, dense ivies and rose bowers and the flow of ocean water all around. This area is essentially peninsular, with an intricate coastline defined by many small coves and inlets. The water views are spectacular. There are thousands of vistas that change continually with the passing day and the mood of the skies. A thick, misty evening can be as electrifying here as a bright sunny day. The harbor is a sailor's mecca during the summer, when tall masts and full sails gamboling in the distance will arouse a sense of marvel, elemental freedom and joyful abandon in even the most dug-in-at-the-heels landlubbing couple. You will have no choice but to gasp with wonderment and embrace.

Note: Bicycles are available for rent here, or bring your own. There is so much to see and be a part of that biking is really the best mode of transportation. Oh, and another thing: Being in this little hamlet often feels like you've traveled back in time to early New England, and yet, at the same time, you'll swear you're in California: Most everyone stops when you're in a crosswalk!

◆ *Second Romantic Option:* Don't miss going to the nearest ocean beach, which is Mecox Beach (in the town of Southampton). Nonresidents pay a hefty parking fee, but it's really a bargain, considering what you get: white silky sand dunes, the entire Atlantic Ocean and each other.

THE AMERICAN HOTEL, Sag Harbor
Main Street
(516) 725-3535
Hotel: Off season — Inexpensive, On season — Expensive
Restaurant: Very Expensive

Use the Long Island Expressway to Exit 70. Go south on Route 111 to Route 27 east to Bridgehampton. Make a left onto County Road 79, which leads straight into Sag Harbor and Main Street. American Hotel is on the right, the last block of Main Street (before the traffic circle and the harbor's Long Wharf).

Calling this place a hotel is like calling Versailles a home. There are only eight rooms here and yet the owner cares for this bed & breakfast hotel and restaurant as if it were a delicate flower, and his dotage is not unwarranted. The eclectically decorated rooms are all oversized. The furnishings are genuine antiques with some deco pieces thrown in, and the mood is an elegant mixture of Victorian and Americana. All is refined and stylish, with decorative touches of whimsy. Everything is fastidiously maintained. Even though so much of it is old, it all seems as if it were finished yesterday, from the stripped doors, exposed brick walls and vintage fixtures to the wood detailing. Each room occupies a corner of the hotel with windows on two walls, and so all are bright. One has a loft bedroom and beamed ceilings. Views are the only thing lacking at the American Hotel, but you're only a block away from everything there is to see.

The dining room is well known and, in a word, superb. The style is elegance applied to a casual, unaffected self-assuredness. Tall tapers on the tables softly brighten the dark wooded room and they glimmer off the abundant crystal. Luncheon is served on weekends, and this is particularly enjoyable in the sun-filled, glass-topped atrium room. The menu is Continental highlighted by such exotic dishes as pheasant mousse.

♦ *Romantic Option:* If being near the ocean is not enough for you, and the sound of the surf at night is an (understandable) romantic must, then the **Sag Harbor Inn, West Water Street, Sag Harbor, (516) 725-2949** (Off season — Inexpensive, On season — Expensive), can fit that requirement. Unremarkable in most every way, this inn is more like a motor lodge. It's newly built and well constructed but lacks any sense of character or style. On the other hand, there is a pool and there are private balconies, lounges and terraces, a third floor promenade deck and, of course, the ocean, which is the only reason you would make a reservation.

SHELTER ISLAND

Via ferry from Sag Harbor and North Haven on Long Island's South Fork. The Greenport Ferry, (516) 749-0139, takes about 10 minutes. The North Haven Ferry, (516) 749-1200, crosses to the island in a mere three minutes.

Shelter Island really is an island, which may not mean much in this part of the world where everything is an island: Manhattan, Long Island, Staten Island, City Island, Roosevelt Island, even Rikers is an island. . . . But Shelter Island is one of another age and genre that embraces you with its feeling of remoteness and privacy because no bridges connect it to anything else. The only way to get there is by boat. This is a timeless place of unhurried quiet, a tattered oak leaf of land caught between the tines of Long Island's forked east end.

First settled in 1652, the island has a New England aura of permanence and charm in its steep wooded hills and bluffs. The coastline is quite intricate, with elusive coves and spits of sand, narrow fingers of land with deserted, impeccable white beaches. Here is an endless scenic adventure, with frequent water views framed by beautiful forests. The roads turn under large stands of oak, past distinguished Victorian homes, creeks, ponds and along the varied shoreline. This dollop of land achieves perfection in its informal amalgam of country and seaside life. If you can, get intimately acquainted with the island by bike, boat or both. And at some point be sure to get to Shore Road in Dering Harbor. On the land you'll see fine, sedate homes; on the water, a fleet that is a veritable boat show. Of course the most important attractions are the misty morning fog, the bright midday sun, the sounds and smells of the sea, the sunrise, the sunset and the moon glimmering on the water at night. Yes, romantic perfection if I do say so myself.

 ◆ *Romantic Option:* Since you came to Shelter Island on one of two ferries (unless you sailed your own boat), take the other ferry and visit the sites to the north or south. If you came through Greenport, take the South Ferry to North Haven and go to Sag

Harbor, the Hamptons and Montauk. If you came from Sag Harbor and North Haven, take the North Ferry to Greenport and explore that village and Orient Point and take in the surviving rural character of the North Fork.

♦ *Romantic Suggestion:* **Mashomack Preserve on Shelter Island, (516) 749-1001,** is a breathtakingly beautiful sanctuary owned by the Nature Conservancy. It is a place unlike most any other in the world, a rare landscape of salt marshes, tidal creeks, fields, woodlands and sandy coastline that is essentially an awesome museum of life in process. The Preserve occupies an entire peninsula of Shelter Island and there are four secluded loop trails of varied length and terrain for the two of you to explore. Unfortunately, there is a warning that goes with some of the nicest places on earth and that is the scourge of warm outdoor activity — ticks. So take all advised precautions, but don't let this stop you from visiting and hiking.

Note: Mashomack is closed on Tuesdays.

RAM'S HEAD INN, Shelter Island   ◆◆◆
Shelter Island Heights
(516) 749-0811
Inn: Inexpensive to Moderate
Restaurant: Moderate to Expensive

Follow the directions to Shelter Island, once on the island, from the South Ferry take Route 114 north to the fork, going straight on Cartright Road to the stop sign. Turn right on Ram Island Drive over the causeway to the Inn on your right. From the North Ferry, take Route 114 south, pass the Mobil station making a left on Winthrop Road, then turn right onto Cobbet's Lane to the dead end. Then take the first left and the next right over the causeway to the Inn.

On the surface this is a simple, gracious country inn sitting atop a hill on a pretty little thumbprint of land stretching into Gardiner's Bay in the tweezers end of Long Island. Big Ram Island is connected,

actually, to Shelter Island by a narrow stretch of land, but in spite
of this, or because of it, The Ram's Head Inn is two worlds removed
from the everyday. The 1927 center hall colonial-styled structure
that the Inn occupies is not overwrought with designer touches. Its
manner is understated, so that the place feels familiar without being
cloying, and formal without being stuffy. The seventeen rooms and
suites have either private or shared baths and all are on the second
floor, where the sound of the rustling leaves and branches from the
magnificent oaks that cloak the Inn is all the music you may need
during your stay. Here the best things are outdoors; the area is
surrounded by sweeping lawns and flowering shrubs, and the view
from the dining area, covered terrace, flagstone patio and lounge
descends across the yard to the harbor for spectacular sunsets. There
are two sloops for guest use, 800 feet of private beachfront, a tennis
court, hammocks, boat moorings and a dock. Continental breakfast
is included and the large dining room and lounge are subtly lit. In
chilly weather the fireplaces provide more than enough warmth, and
the country French menu is wonderful.

◆ *Romantic Option:* **The Dering Harbor Inn, 13 Winthrop
Road, Shelter Island, (516) 749-0900** (Expensive to Very Expensive), has a wonderful location overlooking the harbor and is actually,
and I quote a very romantic source, *"quite exquisite."* It was closed
when we were there for a visit, but from all appearances, it met all
of our criteria for a romantic location.

MONTAUK and the SOUTH FORK

*Take the Triboro Bridge out of Manhattan and follow the signs to Eastern
Long Island. You can choose the Long Island Expressway, the Southern
State Parkway or the Northern State Parkway. Eventually you'll wind up
on Route 27, which takes you directly into Montauk.*

Like most natives, after time in and around New York, your hearts
will have the need to escape to a deserted beach. You've heard about

the fabulous, intoxicating eastern coast: white, wide, awesome, sandy
beaches designed for hand-in-hand walks. Well the South Fork
provides all of that and more. Besides, the idea of being on the edge
of the world together New York-style is not to be missed for any reason.

The trip to the very tip of Long Island where Montauk is to be
found, is a historical potpourri, as well as an archaeological treat (and
retreat). Any one of the towns along the way — Westhampton,
Quogue, Hampton Bays, Southampton, Bridgehampton, East
Hampton, Amagansett (among others) and finally Montauk, can
provide everything a city weary couple could ask for. Each of the
towns has its own flavor as do the beaches that grace them. You
might leave the main road at Westhampton and find the gazebo on
the green or the town marina behind Main Street. Both are perfect
places for a picnic or a stroll. After lunch you could follow the signs
to the beach and discover the miles of fabulous new homes facing
the sea on Dune Road. This road runs along the beach all the way
to viewing distance of Southampton. There you can see the results
of the 1937 hurricane, Shinnecock Inlet, and have access to a beach
of extraordinary beauty and a view of the sea that is truly wondrous.
Next you could take the bridge back to the mainland and head in to
Southampton to experience Job's Lane, the oldest street in all of New
York State, filled with lovely, antiquated shops. Or follow the signs
to the beach where you'll find great and grand houses in yesterday's
design and style. The road to follow through Southampton is Route
27A. Continue on this road all the way to the outskirts of Montauk,
where you'll have a choice of 27A or Old Montauk Highway.
Whichever one you take, use the other on the way home.

Once you reach Montauk and pass all the previous locales, the
road becomes more of a lane running alongside the ocean and sand
cliffs. At the end of this peaceful stretch of road lies the remote
outreaches of this town. Void of all the conventions of life back in
the Hamptons, there is only you and the very best nature has to offer
for miles around. This is a place where you learn how to just be
together because, besides from that, there isn't anything else to do.

♦ *Romantic Suggestion:* **The Old Post Inn, 136 Main Street, Southampton, (516) 283-1717** (Off season — Inexpensive, On season — Very Expensive), is an authentic country inn that has been part of the Southampton scene since the original farm house was built in 1684. The Long Island railroad came in the 1850s and brought the first tourists and the first romantic couples to the inn to bask in the comforts of country living. There are seven rooms, all with their own private baths. The common rooms have the original beamed ceilings and glowing fireplaces. Next door to the Inn is the **Old Post House Restaurant, (516) 283-9696** (Moderate to Expensive). This is a perfect romantic spot for dining anytime. There are two fireplaces, the ceilings are low, candles are lit, tablecloths are appropriately lacy and the food is wonderful. Piano music fills the air on Wednesday, Friday and Saturday. (They're open all year round, every day, for lunch and dinner.)

♦ *Second Romantic Suggestion:* **East Hampton** is one of the most beautiful of the towns with this last name. The village itself begins with a pond and ends with a windmill. Park your car and walk around the nearby lanes. Let yourselves get conveniently lost for a while as you discover the 17th-century houses tucked in between the (relatively) more modern ones. If you're in need of refreshment, in the old town hall you'll find the **Barefoot Contessa**, a fresh-food emporium that will weaken your dietary resolve. Whatever you select, it will taste even better when you get to the beach and share it. If you want to stay overnight, there are really only two choices. The first is the **1770 House, 143 Main Street, East Hampton, (516) 324-1770** (Off season — Moderate, On season — Expensive). The seven rooms are beautifully designed with loving detail and an aesthetic flair that is endearing. Breakfast is served in the dining room which is as handsomely decorated as the rest of the home. Besides your morning meal (included in the price of the room) there is a prix fixe dinner menu (Expensive) that features diligently prepared international cuisine every evening. **The Hedges Inn, 74 James Lane, East Hampton, (516) 324-7100** (Off season — Reasonable, On

season — Moderate), is your other option. It is a classic bed &
breakfast with a charming setting, private baths, some rooms with
fireplaces and a very pretty dining setting that serves a very fresh
Continental breakfast and a fairly wonderful American-Italian menu
at night (Moderate to Expensive).

◆ *Third Romantic Suggestion:* There are many options for
lodgings in Montauk: **Gurney's Inn Resort and Spa, Old Montauk
Highway, (516) 668-2345; Montauk Yacht Club and Inn, Star
Island Road, (516) 668-3100;** and the **Panoramic View, Old
Montauk Highway, (516) 668-3000,** to name the three best. They
are indeed beautiful, but they are also fairly popular, massive and
more condoesque than quaint and engaging. If it weren't for the
ocean and surf on this remote point, you wouldn't necessarily know
you had left the city behind.

◆ *Romantic Warning:* Unfortunately, except for seaplanes and
other private charter flights, the infamous Long Island Expressway is
the most direct way to get to the east end of the Island. Well-known
for its bumper-to-bumper traffic at peak hours, the LIE must be treated
with awareness or you'll get off to a most unromantic start. Since
summer weekends start at the end of the work day on Friday and end
Sunday evening, make your trip as pleasant as possible by leaving
the city well before or well after the rush. Staying through till Monday
or leaving on Thursday is an even more romantic traveling alternative.

"TO BE A LOVER IS NOT TO MAKE LOVE,

BUT TO FIND A NEW WAY TO LIVE."

Paul La Cour

◆ New Jersey ◆

Note: *The descriptions that follow are loosely arranged from north to south heading away from Manhattan.*

PALISADES INTERSTATE PARK, Alpine
(201) 768-1360

Drive across the upper level of the George Washington Bridge to Palisades Parkway north. Exit 2, Alpine Closter, is seven miles north. Once off the exit, follow signs to the Alpine Boat Basin.

The park that lines the New Jersey side of the Hudson River along the cliffs of the Palisades is a bastion of country relief astonishingly close to Manhattan. Isolated, varied and rich in history, the Palisades are a gorgeous example of the enclaves of nature that thrive amid the city, giving testimony to the ability of urban and country life to coexist in harmony. You enter at one end leaving the city world totally behind. What you will find inside is green wilderness strewn with surging creeks and hiking trails.

Drive into the boat basin parking lot and pick up a map of the trails that run through the Palisades. Ask for a schedule of activities, too — you might want to return when there's a concert or a crafts fair in the park. At Alpine you can view the yachts, then choose from either the Shore Trail, which hugs the Hudson for more than ten miles, or the Long Path, which is cut into the cliffs that rise hundreds of feet above the water. Six sets of stairs connect the two so that you hike only as far as you wish, then loop back without retracing your steps. With every twist and turn, the trails offer new wonders for your eyes. Notice the hillsides, thick with vines, and stand next to your beloved to watch some waterfalls cascade over moss-covered emerald rocks. Be sure to climb to a lookout point where you can look across the river and the width of the Bronx.

When you're ready for a rest, follow the spurs off the main trails to remote spots of sandy beach, where you can cuddle undisturbed to your hearts' content.

◆ *Romantic Suggestion:* The drive across the **George Washington Bridge** is a glorious experience, but traffic moves too quickly here for you to catch the spectacular view or sneak a kiss. If you want to enjoy this romantic vista, park your car in Manhattan's Washington Heights and walk along the protected pedestrian path. I prefer the south side of the bridge, where on a clear day you can see the Midtown skyscrapers as well as the Hudson River. You can also walk across this passage between the city and New Jersey. The view up here is a complete kaleidoscope of the city. The center of the bridge enables an open view of everything due north and south. You can come face to face with the more serene, magical side of this megalopolis and, for a total change of pace, there will be almost no one up here but you.

PALISADEUM, Cliffside Park
(201) 224-2211
Moderate to Expensive

Take the upper-level of the George Washington Bridge to the Fort Lee Exit. Make three left turns at the next series of intersections until you are on LeMoine Avenue going south. This will become Palisades Avenue. At the fork in the road stay left and soon thereafter, turn left, when you see the sign for the restaurant.

You won't catch my husband and me near one of those heart-shaped, champagne-filled bathtubs in the Poconos (we claim to be too "*sophisticated*" to be persuaded by such tacky, commercial gimmicks). So please don't tell anyone that once in a while we sneak over the GW Bridge for this restaurant, which probably evokes the exact same feeling. When we were seventeen, this is exactly the kind of place we would have described as elegance personified. Now that we're older and wiser we realize that the Palisadeum is hardly elegant, but we have also learned that elegance and romance are not necessarily related. What this restaurant lacks in fine detail, it makes up for in excessiveness. In no way subtle, everything at the restaurant is LARGE: from the giant water goblets to the grandiose (faux) fireplace to the golden wine buckets, from the sweeping views of New York City to the flaming Baked Alaska, from the mirrored ceilings to the very-high-backed circular booths. To say the least, this place is obvious in its attempt to impress.

It's important to go to the Palisadeum on an off night when it is not crowded or catering to singles and you will be seated in a private booth near the window. Many of the items on the menu are built for two and are prepared tableside. The portions are huge and the food is good. The desserts, on the other hand, are superb. Consider sampling the Chocolate Grand Marnier souffle, which needs to be ordered along with the main meal. If it is late in the evening or not crowded, you can take your sweets and cappuccino out to the porch where the view is truly astounding.

Note: Depending on your preference there is ballroom-type dancing in the lounge after 8 p.m. (There is only valet parking.)

THE PARK in the TOWN OF WEEHAWKEN

Go through the Lincoln Tunnel right into the Hoboken Tunnel. At the first light turn left and at the next light turn left again onto Boulevard East. Stay on Boulevard East through Weehawken; you'll see the park on the right. There's also a ferry from the pier near the Javitz Center that will take you right there. The ferries run between two points in Weehawken (Lincoln Park and Port Imperial) and 38th Street in New York, Monday through Friday, 6:45 a.m. to 10:30 p.m. Call (201) 902-8850 for ferry information.

Last night I announced to my husband that we were going off in search of yet another romantic nightspot. We commiserated over the fact that there is very little to do at night if, say, one (or two) doesn't want to eat or drink. That's what we were discussing as we passed through the Lincoln Tunnel straight into Wonderland. If you think New York ends at the Hudson River, you've never been to Weehawken. It's at times like these I'm thrilled with the job of searching out and experiencing romantic places. How could I have lived so long in New York and never thought to see what it looked like from the most maligned state in the country? After sunset my husband and I gazed out from the park overlooking the sparkling clear view of Manhattan that spread from the GW Bridge to the Statue of Liberty. We agreed that we would come here many more times and that we would reluctantly share our secret. You want more of a description? Well that would be as effective as describing the *Mona Lisa.* It's a long rolling park along the Hudson, there are benches, green lawn . . . Oh, forget the description, just go there.

SHANGHAI RED'S, Weehawken
Pier D-T
(201) 348-6628
Expensive

From Lincoln Tunnel, turn right into Hoboken Tunnel. Make the first left and then another left at the next light. At the second light, turn right onto Baldwin Avenue. Follow to Shanghai Red's in Lincoln Harbor. Commuter ferries run between two points in Weehawken (Lincoln Harbor and Port Imperial) and 38th Street in New York, Monday through Friday, 6:45 a.m. to 10:30 p.m. Call (201) 902-8850 for ferry information.

The question was whether to give this remarkable restaurant, which gives the illusion of personally owning the New York skyline, its own space in this book or to include it as a romantic option along with the park in Weehawken. The decision is obvious, because even if Shanghai Red's were a two-hour drive from New York rather than a ten-minute one and even if there were no enchanting park to enjoy after or before dinner, it would still be worth the trip.

What a place! The first vision of it, a huge mansion of weathered wood designed to resemble a shack against the mighty backdrop of New York City, seems an impossible dichotomy — and it is. Built on a pier right in the middle of the Hudson, Shanghai Red's is the kind of magic shack that you'd find at Disneyland. With its ten dining rooms, hundreds of antiques, hammocks and farm tools hanging from rafters, warm lounges and blazing fireplaces, it can appear — if you don't look too closely — to be charmingly rustic. On closer inspection, however, it really is a high-tech, opulent fantasy. Regardless of its inauthenticity, the restaurant is indeed glorious, and the breathtaking views that abound from every room and the delicious, artfully prepared food are the things fabulous evenings out are made of.

♦ **Romantic Option:** The restaurant houses a cabaret which changes its atmosphere each night, catering sometimes to rock 'n' rollers and other times to those who love to dance to a Latin beat. There is a separate admission to the cabaret, which can be peeked at through a window in the cocktail lounge.

♦ **Romantic Warning:** Shanghai Red's is a popular place, and for Friday and Saturday nights, reservations are sometimes required a month in advance.

BINGHAMTON'S, Edgewater
725 River Road
(201) 941-2300
Inexpensive

From Manhattan drive through the Lincoln Tunnel and exit at Boulevard East Weehawken. Turn right onto 60th Street, which becomes River Road.

For 62 years, the *Binghamton* carried passengers and automobiles across the Hudson from Hoboken to lower Manhattan and back again. The ferry trade sputtered out in the 1960s, but the historic ship has since been painstakingly restored and reopened as a restaurant. If you're seeking an unusual hideaway spot where you can enjoy a leisurely lunch or a late afternoon cocktail, the trip to New Jersey is well worth it.

Although the *Binghamton* now moves only when it is nudged by tides and currents, much of the ship's original detail remains intact. On the upper deck you can lunch in the galley, an airy space surrounded by windows and decorated with well-polished brass, mahogany and stained glass. Wander downstairs to the engine room to view one of the original steam engines, as well as two 1,000-gallon fish tanks. When the weather is fine, you can sit on the portside deck for a view of the New York skyline. A casual afternoon lunch or drink can easily be transformed into a shipboard romance.

◆ **Romantic Warning:** The food is not the *Binghamton*'s strong suit. The chowder and sandwiches are fine, but unless you relish fried foods and seafood awash in sauces, stay away from the so-called fancier entrees. During the week this is as subdued a spot as you could ask for, but on the weekends the scene changes markedly; you might even call the weekend crowd a bit wild, and they dance to all hours. Unless that fits your notions of romance, better stay away on Friday and Saturday nights.

HIGHLAWN PAVILION, West Orange
Eagle Rock Reservation
(201) 731-DINE
Expensive to Very Expensive

From the Lincoln Tunnel take Route 3 west to the Garden State Parkway and get off at Exit 145. Take Route 280 west and get off at Exit 8B. Follow Prospect Avenue for one-half mile and turn right onto Eagle Rock Avenue; 600 feet down and on the left-hand side of the road is the entrance to the Reservation.

This renovated early-century casino at the very top of a mountain offers one of the most spectacular panoramic views of Manhattan — and parts of the Bronx, Brooklyn and Staten Island if you care to look. In its present incarnation as a posh, Mediterranean villa-style restaurant replete with tile floors, antiques, Spanish grillwork and tapestries, the central attraction is the floor-to-ceiling picture window that makes for ethereal city-gazing any time of day or night. The quiet and airy lounge features an extensive oyster bar. The bartenders are friendly and talkative only when you want them to be, and the waitpeople are attentive and easygoing. For as long as you're here, you'll have the giddy feeling of being above it all. JACKETS REQUIRED!

♦ *Romantic Suggestion:* You won't have to go far for a moment (or much more) of privacy as soon as you step out of the restaurant, because you'll be standing in 408 acres of county park. Walk over to the scenic overlook and take in the view without the window. I must confess to a sentimental attachment to this spot because it was there I first kissed my one true love. We didn't care who looked, but if you need a more secluded vista, try walking down one of the many trails and bridle paths which interconnect throughout the park and discover your very own nook and cranny.

SPRING LAKE

From the Holland Tunnel take the New Jersey Turnpike south to Route 78 south to the Garden State Parkway. Take the Parkway south to Exit 98. Pick up Route 34 east to Route 524; follow east to Spring Lake.

This elegant, turn-of-the-century, Victorian seaside resort is a romantic charmer in all respects. It's a marvelously pictorial town for walking or bicycling because nearly every wide avenue is lined with magnificent hotels, cottages, mansions and estates, many of which are historically notable. But that's not all. This place is a favorite of ours because at every other turn is a choice spot for tender interludes. Most dreamlike are the long wooden bridges which span the lake for which the town is named, the gazebos on the peaceful (non-commercial) two-mile boardwalk, and the wide beach itself. You'll never feel crowded, especially in the long off season, and once you've shared a blissful moment here with your significant other, you'll remember it always. There is something about this place that lingers, like the memory of a sunrise over the Atlantic.

◆ *Romantic Suggestion:* If you decide to spend the night here, which I highly recommend you do, there are many wonderful accommodations. Don't miss trying to get reservations at the hundred-year-old **Normandy Inn, 21 Tuttle Avenue, (201) 449-7172** (Reasonable to Moderate), an Italianate villa with colonial revival and neoclassical interiors. All of the rooms have charming private baths and several look out on the blue, flowing, endless ocean. Request the Tower Room for the best view, or rooms 101 or 102 for their unique headboards and canopied beds. The Inn is open all year and is renowned for its hearty, full Irish breakfasts. Bicycles are available, and you can be met at the train or bus station. From March through November, there is a two-night minimum on weekends, and there is a four-night minimum in July and August.

◆ *Second Romantic Suggestion:* From March through December, try the **Ashling Cottage, 106 Sussex Avenue, (201) 449-3553** (On season — Inexpensive, Off season — Inexpensive to Reasonable). This stately Victorian has ten large, airy rooms (eight with private baths, which are always more romantic than shared) and features breakfast with delectable home-baked items. Ask for the room with the sunken bathroom or, for complete privacy, the one with its own entrance and porch. In season Spring Lake has no shortage of restaurants; try the moderately priced **Beach House, 901 Ocean Avenue, (201) 449-9646,** for its excellent fare and view of the ocean and sun-filled sky. But in the off season you'll have to travel to a neighboring locale for a romantic eating spot.

WARNING: Keep in mind the recent, well-documented environmental problems of the Atlantic in this part of the world if your heart is set on salt-water swimming. Hopefully, it was only a one-time problem that won't recur.

LAMBERTVILLE

*Take the Holland Tunnel to the New Jersey Turnpike south. Pick up
Route 78 west to Route 287 south. Head south again on Route 202. Take
Route 29 south along the Delaware River. Turn right at the traffic light
at Bridge Street into the center of town.*

This artists' colony, snugly ensconced on the bank of the Delaware
River, is a unique combination of a colonial town and a European
hamlet with a dash of Greenwich Village, the dash that's provocative
and romantic. It's a cozy town simply to walk in because of its
picturesque beauty, and every inch of street has something very
interesting to look at or step into: antique stores, art galleries, historic
landmarks, restaurants and specialty shops. The shopkeepers are
noticeably friendly. The other pairs of lovers taking in the town won't
notice if you stop and kiss, because chances are they're doing the
same, especially where a particularly exquisite stretch of the wide
river comes into view.

♦ *Romantic Suggestion:* For all of the place's quaint attractiveness,
there is a somewhat hidden gem here which should absolutely not
be missed no matter what the season. I'm referring to the bicycle
path that lies between the river and the Delaware & Raritan Canal
and can be reached by heading just past the Inn at Lambertville
Station. In spring, summer and fall, pack a picnic and hike or bicycle
to your thighs' and hearts' content (the best area is to the south
between Lambertville and the park at Washington Crossing). On
either side of you is a crystalline body of water and, when you see
the impressionistic reflections of the variegated fall leaves or bright
spring flowers on the canal surface, you may have the idea that you're
really in the French countryside. You can cuddle on the grassy bank
because the area is never crowded. In winter, cross-country skiing is
a preferred, thoroughly exhilarating activity.

♦ *Romantic Options:* The town has several inns if you're planning
to stay overnight. The most romantic is the **Coryell House Bed &
Breakfast, 44 Coryell Street, (609) 397-2750** (Reasonable),

which features charming antique-furnished rooms and a country-styled breakfast served in bed. Reserve well in advance. Other places, such as the **Bridgestreet House, 67 Bridgestreet, (609) 397-2503** (Inexpensive), and the **Inn at Lambertville Station, (800) 524-1091** (Moderate to Expensive), offer more units but aren't quite as private. Among the many places to dine, my favorite is the **Full Moon Restaurant, 23 Bridge Road, (609) 397-1096** (Inexpensive), where the cuisine is always excellent and the service perfectly paced. Be advised, however, that it's closed on Tuesdays and only serves dinner on Fridays and Saturdays. For an aperitif, try the secluded **Boathouse, 8 1/2 Coryell, (609) 397-2244** (Reasonable), just off Coryell Street. The reception desk at the Inn at Lambertville Station provides maps of the town and surrounding area.

DELAWARE WATER GAP
NATIONAL RECREATION AREA

From the George Washington Bridge take Route 80 west to the Delaware Water Gap.

As soon as the magnificent Kittatinny Ridge of the Appalachian Mountains rises up before you, you know without a question that you're coming into direct contact with the vast grandeur of nature. There are 70,000 acres of it in this dynamic park and exciting activity to go along with it in every season. Hiking and sightseeing are possible all year round, and there are so many trails and paths that you can pick and choose to suit your energy levels. In the summer, bring your swimsuit for an aquatic dip in Sunfish Pond, or trek up a hill, find a generously shady tree, unpack your picnic basket and sit back and watch the hawks glide soundlessly below. If you prefer, rent a canoe, hop in, relax and commune with the blue vaults above.

If it snows here, pack the cross-country skis. Be prepared for brisk strides that take you across the crunching snow-packed ground and past trees dressed in white. Regardless of what you choose to do, you'll find the park a perpetual nature study: you might see anything, including deer, fox, birds and yes, even the elusive mink, coyote and black bear. Most important of all, you and your partner will never have a problem with a private kiss in this park because of its size and secluded vistas. In fact, it is the only outdoor location to receive a four-lip rating — you are guaranteed that much privacy.

Note: For comprehensive and expert advice on what to do and where in the park to do it, consult the rangers at the **Kittatinny Point Information Center, (201) 496-4458**, which is on Route 80 near the toll bridge that crosses the Delaware River into Pennsylvania. They're friendly, courteous and eager to help, not to mention full of excellent suggestions.

♦ *Romantic Warning:* After once spending a few hours driving all around the park with my husband in earnest (read desperate) search for a cup of coffee, I learned my lesson and brought my own provisions on subsequent trips. There is also an absence of inns or bed & breakfasts, although the park's historic buildings are slated for conversion into such in the near future.

"DON'T MISS LOVE, IT'S AN INCREDIBLE GIFT."

Leo F. Buscaglia

♦ Miscellaneous New York State ♦

Note: *The descriptions that follow are loosely arranged from south to north heading away from Manhattan.*

THE DONALD M. KENDALL SCULPTURE GARDENS, Purchase

From Manhattan, take the Hutchinson River Parkway north to the exit for Route 120 north (Purchase Street). Go one mile and turn right onto Anderson Hill Road. The Gardens are located at the Pepsico building on your right a mile down Anderson Hill Road.

A nude couple dances wildly in a clearing in the woods. A marble bear guards a graceful pond that's home to cranes and geese. An absurdly giant trowel stands at the edge of an expansive lawn. What a kissing place! And it is also a corporate headquarters. In the Westchester town of Purchase, the Pepsico Company has created perhaps the most romantic setting ever for a weekend stroll or picnic. This is truly a special place to share a combination of nature, art and each other's company. Paths wind through 112 magnificent land-scaped acres, past forty works by noted 20th-century artists like Calder, Miro and Dubuffet. There's a piece for every mood and taste — from the dramatic *Eve* by Rodin to sensuous abstracts and fanciful works of etched creations. The plantings here are exceptionally beautiful as well. There are groves of birch trees, waterlily ponds, exotic trees and plants and seasonal blooms. The gardens are rarely crowded. For extra privacy, try the woodchip paths through the surrounding woods to the right of the main entrance. Three small courtyard gardens in the center of the building complex offer moments alone, too.

Note: The grounds are open every day during daylight hours. There are also a handful of picnic tables beside the pond.

TARRYTOWN

Take the Henry Hudson Parkway to Route 9 north into Tarrytown.

Ever since the early explorers sang the praises of the Hudson River Valley centuries ago, travelers have been drawn to Tarrytown. It certainly offers everything you can think of: cultural attractions, rich history and beautiful scenery, with ubiquitous views of the surging river. And yes, romance. Of course some Tarrytown locations are more amorous than others, and they are well worth seeking out. At the very top of my list is **Lyndhurst, 635 South Broadway**, the luxuriant 67-acre estate that once belonged to railroad magnate Jay Gould. The centerpiece of this manor is the breathtaking Gothic Revival mansion (which can be toured with a guide, although it's preferable to go it alone), but what surrounds it is what will steal your breath away: rolling hills and sweeping lawns, groves of stately trees, abundant foliage, rocks and rose gardens. As you look over these august grounds, you're the reigning royalty of your own kingdom. Spread a picnic and breathe deeply the fragrant air. Enjoy a delicious moment in the gazebo off the rose garden or simply watch the river flow.

If you prefer literary opulence, take Route 9 south from the center of Tarrytown and follow the signs to Sunnyside, the somewhat smaller estate of the legendary author Washington Irving. The house itself can be toured in the company of costumed guides, and the gently undulating grounds feature ponds, gazebo, picnic benches, exquisite greenery and, of course, winding pathways with views of the Hudson River, which Irving called the most incomparable in all his wide travels. At either place, the murmurs from the river drift into your ears and lull you into the consummate fantasy of country living.

Note: Lyndhurst is open to the public May 1st through October 31st, and December, Tuesday through Sunday, 10 a.m. to 5 p.m.; January through April and November, weekends, 10 a.m. to 5 p.m. Closed on holidays.

◆ **Romantic Option:** If you are in the mood for more solitude, explore the 750-acre **Rockefeller State Park Preserve** in Pocantico Hills just above North Tarrytown (take Route 9 north to Route 117 east to the park entrance). Here you'll find a luscious network of shady river lanes, intimate wooded paths and panoramic vistas. Permits are available for horseback riding and carriage driving. If it snows, pack your cross-country skis.

◆ **Romantic Suggestion:** The perfect conclusion to the perfect day can be found at **Isabel's, 61 Main Street, Tarrytown, (914) 631-6819** (Inexpensive to Moderate). The atmosphere is extremely cozy and the ambience endearing. The specialty here is dinner and snacks. The wine and cheese menu is extensive.

TAPPAN HILL RESTAURANT, Tarrytown
81 Highland Avenue
(914) 631-3030
Expensive

Major Deegan Expressway (87 north) to Exit 9. Turn right onto Route 119. At first traffic light turn left onto Benedict Avenue. At the fourth traffic light turn right onto Highland Avenue. Make a left at the stop sign.

Mark Twain once owned this estate perched in the heights of posh Tarrytown. Now it is a mecca for lovers of food, beauty and each other. Arrive in winter and you'll be welcomed by fireplaces blazing in the mansion's regal vestibule and adjoining cocktail lounges. The profusion of lights conspire to replace those chills with a toasty glow of expectation. In the summer months the area is full of enchantment. Walk the verdant promenade that leads from the restaurant to a semicircular second tier and watch the sun descend over the powerful waterway below.

It's worth the wait for a window table in the spacious dining room; the unobstructed view of the Hudson River and Palisades is stupendous. You'll savor the panoramic splendor over good and often delicious contemporary American food served with hospitality and elegance. Steak, fresh fish, rack of lamb are all impressively prepared, and the award-winning espresso fudge cake is itself worth a trip.

♦ **Romantic Suggestion:** It's summer and the Westchester air is cool and fragrant. Why return to the stifling city? Or it's winter and the ground out here is blanketed in pure white drifts of snow, so why return to a slushy frozen city? A few minutes away the **Tarrytown Hilton, 455 South Broadway, (914) 631-5700** (Moderate to Very Expensive), offers excellent accommodations at low weekend rates. Not the height of romantic sleeping arrangements, but it can be more so than returning to the city. This Hilton also has a nice restaurant and a delectable brunch on Sundays.

ROCKLAND LAKE STATE PARK
(914) 268-7598

Take the George Washington Bridge to Palisades Parkway. At Exit 4 turn onto Route 9W north. Stay on Route 9W until you see a sign for Rockland Lake South entrance.

A fumy turnpike or a dark, thronged tunnel can threaten romance right at the start of your excursion out of New York City, but the 40-minute drive to Rockland Lake will be scenic and serene. The tree-lined Palisades is fast and Route 9 affords enchanting glimpses of the Hudson River and Tappan Zee Bridge as you pass through the appropriately named town of Grandview.

The 2.8-mile path that winds around the lake is paved and flat, posing no obstacles to the exchange of soulful thoughts. As the vista changes subtly with each curve, you'll marvel at the tranquility and freshness so close to a bursting metropolis. Scattered among the lakeside trees are grassy nooks, some with benches and tables. Although the seclusion is far from utter solitude, a cuddly, discreet picnic would not be out of place or easily observed. You can rent a rowboat at the ducks' gathering place and float through your surroundings.

◆ **Romantic Warning:** At least one of the park's two swimming pools is open on weekends from Memorial Day to Labor Day. A June dip will enliven the senses, but once school is out, stay away! Those romantic urges will wither with the first chlorine-bound tot's cries of delight.

◆ **Romantic Suggestion:** Wear outfits that can be dressed up so that you can take advantage of the lovely **Bully Boy Chop House, 117 SR 303, (914) 268-6555** (Moderate to Expensive). It is a Rockland gastronomic gem just minutes away. Be sure to reserve a table overlooking their pond for a perfect backdrop to a British-inspired feast. Scones with honey, succulent curried beef and savory rack of lamb are among the pleasures of the cordially served bounty.

ISABELLE'S at HIGH TOR VINEYARDS, New City
100 High Tor Road
(914) 638-3204
Moderate to Expensive

Take the George Washington Bridge to Palisades Parkway. Exit 12 to Route 45N. Shortly thereafter take a right at the Conklin Orchards onto South Mountain Road. Follow the signs to High Tor Vineyards.

To reach High Tor you'll snake along south Mountain Road through the loveliest rural landscape then branch off at the marker to ascend a one-lane passage to your secluded destination.

While the winery is open for touring only in August and September, you can sample its products throughout the year on weekends from 11 to 5. In the tasting room three premium and three table wines as well as a sherry are amiably proffered; it's not the Napa Valley but . . .

Our real objective is Isabelle's, behind the winery via a cobblestone path. Divided into three small rooms, featuring beamed ceilings, exposed brick, tables sporting white linens and fresh flowers, this picturesque restaurant serves brunch from 11 to 3 every Sunday and seasonally on Saturdays. (Reservations are prudent.) In the winter you'll be surrounded by snowy woods and warmed by a crackling fire. But the outdoor terrace is especially felicitous for summer dining: a stream flowing alongside, birds in song and awash in the fragrance of roses.

The menu includes omelettes, chicken, fish and pasta complemented by the house vintages. Service is casual and leisurely. It's easy to linger through the afternoon sipping *"Rockland White,"* lulled by the evocative harmonies of the flute-guitar duo.

◆ **Romantic Option:** After brunch and a wine sampling, get back on the Palisades and continue north to **Bear Mountain, (914) 786-2701.** Though this scenic area draws a crowd, a stroll around **Hessian Lake** is always renewing and there are more than 5,000 emerald acres in which you can easily find an area all to yourselves.

COLD SPRING

Take the Palisades Parkway north to Bear Mountain Bridge and turn left on Route 9D. Travel nine miles on 9D farther north to Cold Spring (not to be confused with Cold Spring Harbor on Long Island). Once in Cold Spring turn left on Main Street to the end. Looking past the train tracks you'll see the Hudson River in front of you, but the car can't cross the tracks here, so follow the signs, which will take you around the block to the water. Park your car there at the public boat-launching ramp.

Start your day in Cold Spring right there in the company of giant graceful white swans, ducks and sea gulls. To them you'll look just like everyone else they see every day locked in a sweet embrace, looking out over the water and breathing in the clean air. Perhaps take a walk along the water one block to the **Dockside Harbor Restaurant, (914) 265-3503** (Moderate). Wipe the lipstick from your sweetheart's cheek and have lunch or make your way back to Main Street (pedestrians can go through a tunnel under the tracks).

The quaint little town is an antique and craft admirer's paradise.

♦ *Romantic Suggestions:* Although Cold Spring is close to New York and can be enjoyed comfortably as a day trip, there are so many things to see and do here that you couldn't go wrong making a weekend of it. Besides shopping, two special outdoor sites are the **Boscobel Mansion Restoration and Gardens in Garrison, (914) 265-3638,** and **Constitution Marsh Sanctuary, (914) 265-3119.** Two of our favorite bed & breakfasts are the **Plumbush Inn, Route 9D, Cold Spring, (914) 265-3904** (Moderate), which also serves superb European-styled food and has wonderfully appointed rooms, one with private bath, and the **Pig Hill Bed & Breakfast, 73 Main Street, (914) 265-9247** (Moderate). Also, **The Olde Post Inn, 43 Main Street, Cold Spring, (914) 265-2510** (Inexpensive), an 1820 landmark building which is a delightful bed & breakfast with a very unromantic name, has a basement tavern open from 8 p.m. until 1 or 2 a.m. where jazz musicians play on Friday and Saturday nights. (The inn only has shared baths, which explains its inexpensive rating. Not a romantic preference, but an economic one.) **Xaviar's, Highland Country Club on Route 9D in Garrison, (914) 424-4228** (Expensive), is quite highly recommended for very special personal occasions. The Continental menu includes fresh venison and rabbit creatively prepared and served in a truly romantic setting. For a very out-of-the-way interlude the **Bird and Bottle, Route 9, Garrison (914) 424-3000** (Moderate to Expensive), is an elegant but rustic colonial home set in the woods. In addition to a restaurant it is also a romantic inn with a well-tended fireplace in your appealing, comfortable room. They have a package price that includes dinner and breakfast for two.

♦ *Romantic Option:* Don't go home without making a stop at **Garrison's Landing.** In fact, this is best enjoyed as a detour on your way to Cold Spring rather than on your way home. When you get on 9D (coming from New York) turn left at the blinking light (Route 403) to the artists' colony that is Garrison. Walk behind the houses, and be sure to take in the view of West Point from the Gazebo. You'll probably see an artist or two entranced in the process of creation. Everywhere you'll see evidence of their work. Stop in at the Art Center, too, before you leave.

GASHO, Central Valley
Route 32
(914) 928-2277
Expensive to Very Expensive

Take the New York State Thruway (87) to Exit 16, Harriman. Bear right after the toll booth. Make a right on Route 32. Gasho is about a mile away, on your left. Approximate driving time: 75 minutes.

Our New York frenetic pace began to soften as soon as we turned into the Gasho property. Driving over a brook, then uphill on a long stately lane, we were soothed into a receptive mood for our arrival at this ancient Japanese estate. Gasho is a replication of a classic 15th-century Japanese farmhouse. While the ample wooden building is rustic, impressive and very unusual, the grounds are an absolute knockout. Take a leisurely stroll around Gasho's five acres. Tarry at the large fish pond, the authentic water mill and the wooden bridge. The classic Japanese gardens are especially beguiling.

The two of you can be alone outside, but don't expect solitude at dinner. What you will get, though, is a sensualist's pleasure, in the restaurant-as-theatre vein. Gasho trains its staff to perform wizardry on steaks, seafood and chicken. Every table seats eight around a steel hibachi, at which your chef prepares fresh food with flair and flavor. Watching my mate's firm scallops nestle on the grill against my fresh pink swordfish was a flirtatious promise of things to come.

◆ *Romantic Suggestion:* If you can't bear to leave, consider staying overnight at Gasho's lodge, or cottages, where rates are inexpensive. You could wake up to all this beauty, calm and space. While in the area you will have time to visit nearby **Bear Mountain**, wonderfully romantic (only ten miles away), and the **Storm King Art Center**, an immense sculpture park, in Mountainville (ten miles away).

♦ **Romantic Warnings:** Gasho is packed on weekends, so make reservations. The last seating is at 9:30 p.m. Dress is casual, but wear layers as those grills give off a lot of heat. The drive from Manhattan has several tolls; be sure to bring dimes and quarters.

LAKE MINNEWASKA STATE PARK  (914) 255-0752

Take the New York Thruway (87) north to Exit 18. Turn left on Route 299 and go through the town of New Paltz. Continue to the end and turn right on Route 44-55. Follow the road up the mountain, about four miles past the hairpin turn. Turn left into the park. Pick up a map at the gate; then continue up the windy bumpy road to the parking lot near the lake.

The lake is only ninety miles from New York City, but it might as well be ninety-million. Your first view of the water will be through the trees. The water at first will appear emerald green, but as you draw nearer it will become turquoise. Both colors are astounding from any perspective. But even more than the color, the clean, clear water has a magical quality; swimming in it is like swimming in silk. There are no fish, just an occasional scuba diver exploring the 100-foot-deep bottom of this glacial lake. The lake is said to have a high copper content, which accounts both for its color and lack of fish.

Don't miss taking a walk around the lake trail that winds up and around the white cliffs presiding over half the lake, and don't hesitate to try a few side trails, where it's not unusual to see a deer or two. You may also want to take a rowboat or a paddle boat out on the lake. The park closes at 5 p.m. but be sure to reserve at least one hour to take the easy one-mile walk to Beacon Hill, very probably the most restful spot there is with a spectacular mountain view close to New York City.

♦ **Romantic Option:** There's a cascading waterfall called **Awosting Falls** which you can dip your feet into from above or swim in beneath. It is just inside and near the entrance to Minnewaska State Park, but wait until you're leaving the park to see it, or you may never get to Lake Minnewaska.

♦ *Romantic Warning:* Until recently the park was owned by a family. Now the state owns it. Although they are maintaining the beautiful grounds, they have restricted swimming to a very small area, making it somewhat less pleasurable than in the old days when swimmers could go where they pleased.

♦ *Romantic Suggestion:* If you're spending more than one day in the area, here's an excursion idea, but it's for serious hikers only. **Lake Awosting** (not to be confused with the falls mentioned above) can only be reached by taking a 4.5 mile (each way) hilly path. One of two such paths begins from Minnewaska and is on your map. Along the way there are some little waterfalls and running brooks on the left just off the path. The water at Awosting is not as blue as Minnewaska's, but early in the swimming season it is remarkably clean and clear. Like Minnewaska, Awosting is surrounded by white cliffs and plateaus, one of which juts out into the water and serves as a beach where there is usually a lifeguard on hot summer days (otherwise there's a ranger enforcing no-swimming rules). Along with the lifeguard and a few hearty souls like yourselves, you're sure to bask in the beauty, peace and privacy that will make the rigorous trip worthwhile.

BAKER'S BED & BREAKFAST, Stone Ridge
80 Old Kings Highway
(914) 687-9795
Inexpensive to Moderate

From Lake Minnewaska State Park, turn left on Route 44-55 to the end. Turn right on Route 209 and right again when you get to Old Kings Highway. One hundred yards on the right is the Baker's 210-year-old stone house.

Just off of a main road, the Baker's grounds are surprisingly pastoral and picturesque, and the inn is situated perfectly to take advantage of many recreational sights in the area, including Lakes Minnewaska, Mohonk and Awosting and the towns of Stone Ridge, Woodstock, Kingston and New Paltz. The Baker's will welcome you with a glass of wine or cider. Each room (some with half-baths, some with full) is decorated in antiques and equipped with down comforters, and each has its own charm. And, unlike many bed & breakfasts, most guests feel comfortable roaming about the many common areas of the house, including a game room, a living room, a solarium with hot tub, a dining room, a breakfast nook and a very comfortable and private television corner. In the back of the house is an expanse containing a vegetable garden, a tiny lily-padded pond with a raft, and a lazy hammock big enough for two (well, maybe one and a half). Breakfast by your hostess is too good to be described, but suffice it to say the vegetable garden is not just for show, and breakfast will usually hold one for most of the day.

Note: There is a two-night minimum and no children allowed on weekends. At all times there is no smoking and no pets.

♦ ***Romantic Suggestions:*** Located nearby in the town of High Falls is the four-star **De Puy Canal House Restaurant, (916) 687-7700** (Moderate to Expensive). Like the Baker's, it is an old stone house with many rooms filled with antiques and blazing fireplaces. We have dined there many times, and more than once we have been seated in our own such room (although this is very unlikely on a weekend, when reservations are strongly recommended). The food is exceptional and the multi-courses have been known to take four hours, but guests are encouraged to roam about the beautiful mansion while awaiting courses and there are several interesting spots for embracing and kissing. One such spot is a catwalk which overlooks the sparkling clean kitchen; you'll discover the others.

Or dine at the Baker's own **1820 Inn Restaurant** just two miles down the road from their B & B. It's almost worth the two-hour trip from New York just for dinner or breakfast, but do yourselves a favor and make a weekend of it.

"TO WRITE A GOOD LOVE LETTER, YOU OUGHT TO
BEGIN WITHOUT KNOWING WHAT YOU MEAN TO SAY,
AND TO FINISH WITHOUT KNOWING WHAT
YOU HAVE WRITTEN."

Jean Jacques Rousseau

YOUR OWN PERSONAL DIARY

This is the section just for the two of you, so you can keep your own record of the romantic, fulfilling moments you've shared together — where you went, what you discovered, the occasion celebrated and whatever else you want to remember long after the weekend, evening or morning has passed. Keeping a record of special times together to read to each other when the moment is right can be an adoring gift, at a quiet moment, sometime in the future, when another magic-filled romantic outing is at hand.

"COMPARED TO OTHER FEELINGS, LOVE IS AN
ELEMENTAL COSMIC FORCE WEARING A DISGUISE OF
MEEKNESS . . . IT IS NOT A STATE OF MIND:
IT IS THE FOUNDATION OF THE UNIVERSE."

Boris Pasternak

"LOVE, WITH VERY YOUNG PEOPLE, IS A HEARTLESS BUSINESS. WE DRINK AT THAT AGE FROM THIRST, OR TO GET DRUNK; IT IS ONLY LATER IN LIFE THAT WE OCCUPY OURSELVES WITH THE INDIVIDUALITY OF THE WINE."

Isak Dinesen

"LOVE IS THE TRIUMPH OF
IMAGINATION OVER INTELLIGENCE."

H.L. Mencken

INDEX

◆ New York City ◆

♦ Worth The Trip ♦

"IT IS OVERDOING THE THING TO DIE OF LOVE."

Anonymous

> "TO BE IN LOVE IS MERELY TO BE IN
> A STATE OF PERPETUAL ANAESTHESIA."
>
> *H.L. Mencken*